THE STATE OF HPC CLOUD

2017 Edition

Nicole Hemsoth, Timothy Prickett Morgan

Next Platform Press

The State of HPC Cloud, 2017 Edition

Copyright © 2017 by Next Platform Press, an imprint of Stackhouse Publishing

Book & Cover Design by Pamela Trush, Delaney-Designs.com

All rights reserved. This book, or parts thereof, may not be reproduced without express permission.

First Print Edition, January, 2017

ISBN: 978-0692836187

Table of Contents

Editors' Introduction 7

Guest Introduction, Leo Reiter 11

Chapter One
   Market Dynamics for HPC Cloud............................17

Chapter Two
   Barriers and Boons for HPC Cloud 25

Chapter Three
   Build Versus Buy: The Perpetual Question for HPC ...77

Chapter Four
   Analysis of Major Public Clouds 91

Chapter Five
   The HPC to Machine Learning Cloud Leap 149

Chapter Six
   The Truth About HPC Cloud—And What's Next....165

References and Resources 169

Editors' Introduction

Welcome to this introductory edition of the *State of HPC in the Cloud*, published by Next Platform Press.

In this 2017 edition, we will outline key trends in high performance computing in the cloud as well as provide remarks on the overall status of cloud computing more broadly.

While this is the first time an edition is being published around this topic, the editors of this book have been closely following cloud computing at scale and high performance computing since those two areas came together around 2008. What is clear is that adoption might not be as wildly enthusiastic as some thought in the early days, but there are new HPC cloud use cases added to the ranks each month. These are driven by new advances in hardware and software and a broader recognition by the ISV community that HPC codes need usage models that extend past on-premises licenses.

The last year has also been one of great change in terms of HPC cloud, in part because of the wave of interest in deep learning and machine learning. These developments have pushed cloud vendors to mix up their hardware and software approaches by adding accelerators that were once most valuable for HPC workloads, which has in turn been a great benefit to future HPC clouds.

To provide insight into the overall ecosystem, we begin with a market analysis of where HPC in the cloud stands, highlighting the role of this unique set of workloads against the larger backdrop of enterprise cloud computing. We then look at the barriers and positive directions to make these market dynamics more favorable in the years to come by looking at issues including software licensing, the availability of accelerators and high speed networking gear, and some key security, compliance, and other developments. We then will move to look at the public clouds more generally before widening out to see where both machine learning and HPC fit.

If there is any theme that we have consistently encountered while crafting this book, it is that specialization matters. Even the large cloud providers who might have found it difficult to invest in tooling and hardware just for HPC in the early days see that the expertise and specialization could pay off for a new host of applications. In short, for the 2016 edition, specialization of compute and partnerships is the key, as Leo Reiter will discuss in his guest introduction.

Regular readers of our publication will recognize a number of these topics and features. Instead of creating a complete volume from the ground up, we assessed our coverage, analysis, and interviews over the course of the last year and synthesized those ideas into a narrative separated by chapters.

This process itself is interesting because oftentimes, these stories or interviews emerge individually, and in the context of the bigger industry picture, only as introductory or concluding statements. However, by putting our thoughts together into chapter form, we were able to ascertain some very big picture trends for HPC clouds—and cloud computing in general. It is our hope that we have presented this tapestry well and in a manner that provides a specific view into HPC cloud computing in 2016-2017 more generally.

Before launching into the book, we would like to thank our partner, Situation Publishing, publisher of *The Register*, as well as our sponsor for the free download week of the book, Nimbix, a provider of specialized cloud computing focused on those special needs for HPC we just spoke of.

Once again, thank you for your interest in both the book and your continued readership at *The Next Platform*.

Nicole Hemsoth, Co-Founder and Co-Editor,
The Next Platform

Timothy Prickett Morgan, Co-Founder and Co-Editor, *The Next Platform*

Guest Introduction

In a World of General Purpose Cloud, Why Specialization Matters
Leo Reiter, CTO, Nimbix

We live in a world where standardization is the norm with just about every product and service we use--whether it's energy, transportation, or clothing, for example. Imagine what would happen if every electrical device required its own unique power source – our lives would be impossible. Instead, we take for granted that the receptacle has so many prongs, so much voltage, and can handle so much alternating current. While these things vary depending on where we are in the world, they are constant in our regular everyday use.

Our trains are built for tracks of specific gauges, our highways governed by the same set of rules regardless of where they lead, and a "large" shirt fits a certain way, for the most part, regardless of what brand it is. These standards are good and serve the general purpose. As long as we're not trying to power heavy industrial equipment, operate a vintage locomotive from another time, or dress for a reenactment of the signing of the Magna Carta, general purpose generally gets the job done.

But what happens when general purpose is not good enough? Sure, we all appreciate the economies of scale and predictable, utilitarian levels of service, but sometimes we need something more – we need specialization. The neighborhood diner is fine for soup, sandwiches, and pies, but it's probably best to have an experienced *itamae* prepare your favorite *o-toro no sashimi*.

Cloud computing is no different. If general-purpose cloud storage and compute is what you seek, you're in luck because there is plenty - at incredibly low rates. Storage is virtually free when it comes to having a place to put files for later retrieval at least. Compute is very inexpensive when it comes to running web services and lightweight workloads that spend the bulk of their time waiting for user or network input. These services become a problem once you start having to compromise – when the low unit cost is either irrelevant or the number (or type) of units required to get the job done in a reasonable amount of time breaks the economics completely. This is why specialized services do exist. Some computing workloads are more like *o-toro no sashimi* than turkey sandwiches. In fact, a lot of them are, and a lot more will be in the coming years.

We've transitioned from the era of data management to one of data science. We spent the bulk of the 20th century (and early 21st) perfecting the mechanisms needed to store, index, and retrieve large amounts of data. While this was a compute problem early on, it became a bandwidth and latency problem once microprocessors got fast enough to run basic algorithms, such as binary searches, without breaking a sweat. Today, these data mechanisms are as basic as arithmetic instructions were many decades ago, and are a given in any software model. Now, the real innovation is in deriving insight from information. This means analyzing multiple massive unstructured data sources at once (a.k.a. "big data") or building new processes automatically based on prior analytics (a.k.a. "cognitive computing"). And of course, this means the bottleneck now shifts back to compute – in a major way. In fact, the problem is getting worse – once we taste the spoils of data science, our appetite knows no limit. What if we consider more data points? What about more layers?

More variables? You get the picture. Every time we ask such questions, we imply more compute.

And with more compute comes more demands on ancillary systems. For example, if we can process data faster, then naturally we will want to process more data. This means denser storage, higher bandwidth, and lower latency. We will want to parallelize algorithms for quicker (even real-time) results. This means faster (and denser) memory, coprocessors, and interconnects. Data science, especially the cognitive sort (which also extends to machine learning), is the engine that will drive computing innovation from now on. Like any high-performance engine, however, it's thirsty, especially when we put our proverbial right foot to the floor as we will no doubt keep doing.

So how do we service this demand? We have general purpose exascale platforms at our disposal which run millions of workloads per day, at low unit prices. This makes up much of the public cloud. The conventional wisdom is to just string lots of these low-cost instances together and rely on "embarrassingly parallel" algorithms to get the job done. The reality is, however, that most algorithms don't scale that well, nor does the underlying general purpose compute. The more instances you have, the more interconnects cause bottlenecks. Adding more instances in many cases slows things down. If you spend enough time on large computers, you come to learn that nothing scales linearly. Or, another way to put it, "everything scales on the whiteboard." Even if you can scale well enough, you still have to manage all these resources. Public cloud providers bill you whether your instances are fully utilized or not, much like the electric company does when you forget to turn the lights off when leaving a room. General purpose computing, when applied to complex tasks, can easily become more expensive than specialized platforms. But more importantly, there are things general purpose clouds simply can't do.

Computational accelerators, such as GPUs and FPGAs, are essential for complex tasks such as training deep neural networks. GPUs, for example, do one thing really well – simple vector math – and can parallelize these instructions thousands of times more than CPUs can. They are invaluable tools for algorithms benefitting from lots and lots of these simple calculations. Well-written algorithms that take weeks on CPUs may take hours or even minutes on GPUs. General purpose clouds have limited options when it comes to computational accelerators. Part of the problem is their virtualized nature, which makes it difficult to orchestrate and expose high-end resources such as GPUs and FPGAs. But the bigger problem is that these service providers live and die by economies of scale, and tend to deploy resources that are easy to spread across many common workloads at once. GPUs and FPGAs are not good at this, and the models that are typically run on CPUs are not appropriate for high-end workflows due to lack of memory or computational capabilities.

The bottom line is that if the bulk of a service provider's revenue comes from lightweight CPU-only web services, they generally will not invest in vast arrays of computational accelerators for dedicated workloads. They will also typically not invest in the requisite software and support services – high end accelerators are not "plug and play" and thus require purpose-built, vertically integrated platforms (with optimized turnkey workflows) to really exploit their potential. On most cloud platforms you get a "least common denominator" of compute, storage, and network - with some deviations toward higher end resources, but well within the confines of the overall general purpose infrastructure.

Specialized cloud platforms for high-end workloads do two things very differently. First, service providers in this space focus exclusively on these types of workflows – simulation, analytics, and machine learning to name a few. Sure, this is a small subset of the broad information technology market, but still equates to billions of dollars (or more) per year of opportunity. By laser focusing, specialized cloud providers such as Nimbix deliver optimized, vertically integrated platforms to cater to these specific high-end use cases.

Second, specialized cloud providers focus on solution cost rather than unit economics. If you ask someone how much it costs to cool their home in the summer, the answer you're looking for is some average dollar amount for the entire summer, not some price per kilowatt hour. Metaphorically speaking, general purpose clouds sell kilowatt-hours, while specialized clouds are in the business of cooling living rooms. There's a big difference. Specialized cloud providers focus much more on the end user problem than they do on providing the infrastructure and building blocks needed to put together services to later attack those problems. It's the difference between tools and solutions, and it's exactly what we need as the never-ending stream of new and more demanding algorithms come to market. And best of all, while unit prices may be higher on specialized clouds, overall solution costs are significantly lower. In short, specialized clouds allow users to focus exclusively on their domain expertise, not on how to configure and operate cloud platforms themselves. This "democratization without compromise" is the key to unlocking long-term innovation, as, for example, the personal computer did for prior generations.

There is plenty of room for both general purpose and specialized clouds in our world. Most people, businesses, and organizations leverage multiple clouds on a daily basis already, and choosing specialized platforms for high-end workloads versus compromising with lesser resources should be no exception. Our hunger for computing capabilities of all sorts is outpacing its supply, which means we'll continue to see a very diverse ecosystem of cloud computing companies catering to all walks of life.

Chapter One

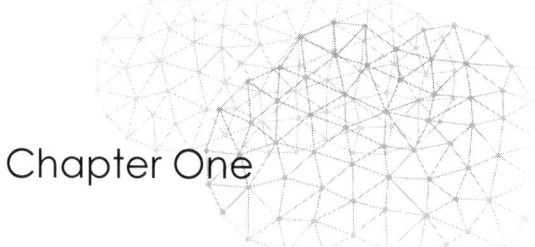

Market Dynamics for HPC Cloud

The behemoths of the IT industry have been talking about running HPC simulations and models in a utility fashion for a lot longer than we have been calling it cloud computing. And the irony is that this is still, despite all of the compelling arguments in favor of HPC in the cloud, a nascent market and one that defies easy qualification and quantification.

We could no doubt find a data processing bureau example from the 1960s or 1970s where a scientific application was run on a paid-for basis without the customer actually owning the iron, but this is not what we mean when we say that HPC in the cloud has been around for a long time.

Back in the fall of 1999 and not only way before it tacked Enterprise onto its name and a few years before it acquired Compaq, Hewlett Packard unveiled its Utility Data Center concept, bringing together a set of virtualization technologies that it acquired from Terraspring and developed in-house at HP Labs to create pools of virtual compute, storage, and networking capacity and a master switch that could dial them up and down over distributed systems; Phillips Electronics and DreamWorks Animation were early customers. IBM started talking up its OnDemand utility computing efforts around the same time, mostly aimed at webscale and enterprise workloads, but fired up its Supercomputing OnDemand utilities in early 2003, with Power and X86 clusters for running HPC applications utility style and with Petroleum Geo-Services being the flagship customer. Sun Microsystems launched the Sun Grid in February 2005, combining its Solaris Unix systems, Java runtime, and Grid Engine workload management, all for a $1 per core per hour flat fee, and got it up and running in March 2006.

That timing for the Sun Grid is significant because that is also when Amazon Web Services was launched, and for all we know, these and other utility-style computing efforts may have collectively been the inspiration that drove the online bookseller and expanding retailing giant to start peddling raw compute and storage capacity as a service. What we can say is that HPE, IBM, and Sun did not get utility computing right, but AWS certainly has and hyperscalers like Microsoft Azure and Google Cloud Platform, hosters turned clouds like IBM SoftLayer and Rackspace Hosting, and upstarts like Nimbix, UberCloud, Sabalcore, and Penguin Computing have all set their sights on attracting traditional HPC (simulation and modeling) and new style HPC (machine learning and accelerated databases) workloads to their cloudy infrastructure.

To try to reckon how much HPC there is in the cloud, by which we mean in both private cloud infrastructure in the corporate datacenter as well as in the public clouds, we have to back into it several different ways, and even then, the error bars on market sizing are probably pretty large. Incidentally, we have exactly the same issues in trying to figure out how much of the infrastructure being sold across the IT industry is cloudy and how much of it isn't (meaning it is traditional bare metal or virtualized infrastructure without sophisticated orchestration and without utility pricing). What can be honestly said is that the definition of cloud keeps evolving and that all infrastructure, in the fullness of time, will eventually be part of an orchestrated, metered, geographically distributed complex of compute, storage, and networking. And by then, we won't call it *cloud* at all. We will call it *computing*, or better still, *data processing* and *data storage*, as we did in the old days.

So first, let's get a handle on overall IT spending and then cloud spending within that. Then we will look at HPC spending as best we can sort it, and then take a stab at what spending on HPC in the cloud is today and what it could be as clouds get more HPC friendly.

According to IDC, worldwide IT spending across all hardware, software, and services (including telecom data services) hit $2.46 trillion in 2015 and, as of the summer, was projected to stay around $2.4 trillion in 2016 and grow to more than $2.8 trillion by 2020. That represents a compound annual growth rate of 3.3 percent between 2015 and 2020. Consumer purchases of gear accounted for about a quarter of the spending in 2015, so wipe away $610 million, leaving $1.85 trillion for corporate IT spending. So that is the big number that cloud spending can never be larger than.

If you drill down to the infrastructure itself and break out spending on storage, services, and switches for private clouds as well as public clouds and contrast it with traditional, non-cloudy infrastructure, you get a better sense of how the cloud transformation is progressing within the corporate IT sector. In its latest projections released in July, IDC estimated that spending on cloudy infrastructure would rise by 15.5 percent to $37.1 billion in 2016, with private cloud expenditures within this slice of the IT hardware pie rising by 10.3 percent to $13.8 billion and public cloud infrastructure spending increasing by 18.8 percent to $23.3 billion. (This is what companies spend to buy the infrastructure, it is not the value they derive through an IT budget for the company or sell as a service to companies if they are a service provider or public cloud.) The interesting bit is that of the $101.4 billion in servers, storage, and switching that will be spent in 2016 for all kinds of infrastructure, 63.4 percent of it, or $63.4 billion, will still be for traditional bare metal or virtualized only gear. Forecasting out to 2020, IDC projects that this traditional IT infrastructure will still account for 53 percent of revenues in 2020 after declining at a 1.4 compound annual rate.

These transitions in the enterprise, academia, and government take time, much more time than it takes at HPC centers or hyperscalers. Total spending on cloudy infrastructure will grow by 13.1 percent compounded annually between 2015 and 2020, according to IDC, hitting $59.5 billion at the end of the forecast and representing 47 percent of total infrastructure sales. Of this cloudy infrastructure spending, $38.4 billion will be for public clouds and $21.1 billion will be for private clouds.

Clearly, then, spending on traditional infrastructure is on the wane and shrinking while the overall IT market is growing at a few points a year. Cloud infrastructure spending is growing six or seven times faster than the overall IT market, and public cloud infrastructure spending is growing at something closer to ten times faster, roughly speaking, between now and the end of the decade.

The cloud services that are deployed on top of this raw infrastructure are growing even faster. According to Synergy Research, which tracks cloud infrastructure revenues closely, sales of IaaS, PaaS, and hosted private cloud services were over $8 billion in the second quarter of 2016, up 51 percent. (The data for the second quarter is the most current because companies are only now reporting their third quarter results as we go to press.) Trailing twelve month revenues for all public cloud and private hosted IaaS and PaaS services hit $28 billion.

In the second quarter, Microsoft doubled its Azure cloud revenues for IaaS and PaaS services, and Google grew even faster at 162 percent. But both are significantly smaller than AWS, as is IBM's SoftLayer, which grew 57 percent and a tad faster than the market at large. The top four cloud providers accounted for 54 percent of the market, and their share of the public cloud pie (if you consider hosted private cloud public) rose by 68 percent. The next 20 providers made up another 25.5 percent of the market and grew their revenues by 41 percent, which is a lot faster than the revenue growth for the IT infrastructure market overall to be sure, which is limping along at a few points growth each quarter, and mainly only because of the heavy buying by cloud builders and hyperscalers. The remaining cloud providers accounted for a smidgen more than a fifth of the market, or about $400 million in revenues, and they grew in aggregate of about 27 percent.

The big are clearly getting bigger, which is what happens in a business that depends so much on scale. But there is always room for niche players who have expertise and a different twist on things, too. The question now is what the next phase in scale will be for clouds, and how much of this might be driven by traditional HPC workloads like modeling and simulation and new HPC workloads like accelerated databases, machine learning, data analytics, risk management, fraud detection, and a broadening definition of high performance computing that itself makes market sizing difficult.

The good news for those who are building cloudy HPC capabilities and for those who will be shopping for them is that the HPC market, like the cloud market, is growing faster than the overall IT market.

Let's use HPC systems as a gauge to measure by. In late 2015, the HPC systems market grew quite a bit faster than IDC expected, and instead of growing somewhere between 7 percent and 8 percent as expected, sales rose by 11 percent to hit $11.4 billion across all classes of machines, from high-end supercomputers all the way down to departmental machines. IDC is projecting a dip to only 4 percent growth this year (still twice as fast as the overall IT market growth), hitting $11.9 billion, and for the forecast period from 2015 through 2020 inclusive, revenues for HPC systems will grow at a compound annual rate of 5.9 percent (about three times faster than the IT sector overall), hitting $15.1 billion.

No one seems to be sure how much HPC workload is actually running in the cloud. In IDC surveys done during the summer of 2015, 25.5 percent of HPC sites reported that they were using public cloud infrastructure for some of their workloads, which is up from 13.6 percent in surveys done in 2011, and customers report that 31.2 percent of their workloads have been deployed on clouds. A lot of this is low hanging fruit – embarrassingly parallel stuff that has small datasets easily moved to the cloud – but these are not insignificant percentages.

IDC does not provide an overall HPC spending figure (including storage, switches, software, support, and such), but Intersect360 Research does. The company reckons that the worldwide HPC market accounted for $28.6 billion in 2015, up 2.7 percent from the prior year, and projects further than HPC revenues will grow at a compound annual growth rate of 5.2 percent between 2015 and 2020 to hit $36.9 billion by 2020.

Now comes the time to make some of our own estimates.

If growth rates persist, public cloud spending on infrastructure and platform services will be around $35 billion or so for all of 2016, and the public cloud providers will spend about $25 billion on infrastructure. That is a ratio of 1.4 to 1 for the value of the services delivered to customers versus the cost of the infrastructure underpinning the service. (These are rough estimates mixing Synergy Research and IDC data as outlined above.) Hold that number for a second.

HPC server spending (which includes related parallel file systems or network file systems) is around $12 billion, including servers and storage, in markets that might be on the order of $58 billion and $38 billion, respectively. Eliminate double counting of storage servers in the broader market, and call it something on the order of $85 billion in server and storage hardware combined. That works out to HPC representing maybe 15 percent of overall server and storage sales worldwide. So it is reasonable to assume, perhaps, that over time, HPC in the cloud could represent the same proportion of cloud IaaS and PaaS sales as it does for hardware sales now, and then grow from there as the definition of HPC (which now includes machine learning and all kinds of accelerated and distributed systems) expands. Hold that 15 percent figure now, too.

As we said above, sales of infrastructure to public clouds are expected to grow from $23.3 billion to $38.4 billion from 2016 to 2020. This implies, at the current ratio outlined above, a revenue stream from public clouds of $53.8 billion in 2020 from the IaaS and PaaS services that ride on this infrastructure. And if HPC can represent the 15 percent of the overall server and storage infrastructure that is sold in 2020, then there is no reason – given the architectural changes that cloud builders are weaving into their clouds such as accelerators and low latency, high bandwidth networks – that it cannot, in theory, eventually represent 15 percent of cloudy services revenues, which would work out to $8 billion.

There is another way to try to back into this. In 2020, slightly more than half of all IT system sales will be for traditional, non-cloud systems and slightly less than half will be for cloudy systems, with about a 30 percent of that overall pie coming from public clouds. If HPC could catch up to the IT market overall, then that would imply that 30 percent of HPC spending on servers and storage could be cloudy, and if the current demands for HPC gear persist, then using IDC's numbers that would be about $4.5 billion worth of servers and storage spending that ends up in the cloud, and using that same 1.4 ratio of cloud infrastructure spending to cloud services revenue generated, that would multiply out to around $6.4 billion in implied HPC IaaS and PaaS sales in 2020. (We don't necessarily think that will happen – this is a thought experiment.)

Suffice it to say, the potential for HPC in the cloud in 2020 is probably an order of magnitude more than such spending today, which at 3 percent of spending according to Intersect360 Research would mean around $850 million in revenues. But then again, the potential has been large for more than a decade. The code, licensing, and datasets for HPC applications and the infrastructure for running those applications on the cloud all had to evolve, and much still needs to be done to reach that potential. But we think this time around, HPC on the cloud is going to work better than it did a decade ago.

In the end, the question is not how many public clouds will be vaporized by the big four or five or six. We also wonder how many of the companies that deploy private clouds that system makers build today will be doing so in five years, or ten? And what of specialists who do HPC as a service and focus on solutions instead of raw technology?

With these options for running HPC workloads in large public clouds, as well as other, more specialized alternatives, there is always the question of when it makes sense to simply keep applications on site or just "burst" out into the cloud for extra capacity when needed. As we will review in the next chapter, the economics, technology, and practical questions here are important ones—and not easy to answer.

Chapter Two

Barriers and Boons for HPC Cloud

For those who have followed the trajectory of HPC cloud over the years, a few facts stand out. First, the market appetite for clouds for supercomputing was not quite as voracious as was expected around 2010. Second, even though the market did grow, as we just discussed, HPC users did not flock to the clouds because there are still some critical barriers.

In this chapter, we will walk through those roadblocks, as well as discuss momentum to move them off the HPC cloud path. In doing so, we will touch on the key barriers of software licensing, the availability of high performance processors, accelerators, and networking gear, and of course, the perennial question of security. Aside from the addition of new processing and higher bandwidth networking available in many public cloud settings, the thorny matters of secure data transmission and use and more flexible licensing have not changed overwhelmingly in the last few years. There are some companies and organizations pushing the envelope in both of those areas, which we will outline in a few moments.

HPC software packages are notoriously expensive and complex bundles of code, which for years have been offered to users via physical dongles and rigid strictures about when, where, and by whom the software can be used. As one might imagine, this is by nature at odds with the way software-as-a service works. For users seeking to free up their infrastructure for other workloads or run remotely as a matter of operating principle, finding the

HPC software capabilities that match the requirement can be difficult. There has been some movement on the part of several vendors over the last couple of years and this, if anything, should be enough to push HPC cloud usage higher.

For those who want to run high performance computing applications in the public cloud, there are limited options, but not for the reasons one might expect. Cloud providers like Amazon, for instance, have gone to great lengths to kick users the right hardware and networks for these applications and the business model for spotty HPC use has been widely discussed as a viable, more desirable alternative to the massive in-house cluster if demand is occasional.

HPC Software Licensing Challenges

As noted, the real problem with bringing HPC applications to the cloud has little to do with roadblocks technology-wise. Rather, it is the thorny problem of software licensing that has stalled HPC cloud adoption with few companies offering HPC software taking the first steps to find a flexible model for pricing that rolls with the on-demand, scalable nature of the cloud.

This is problematic for smaller companies who either want to pop off the workstation for more horsepower or who simply don't specialize in HPC and need to run a quick set of demanding HPC tasks without bothering with on-site hardware. In other words, the ability for smaller companies to quickly onboard with high-end engineering packages they're used to using in a pay-as-you go sort of cloud environment is struck down—leaving smaller companies who have hit a workstation wall but that have large-scale simulations to run with the decision to either procure and maintain a power-hungry cluster or use an HPC on demand service, which is less nimble scalability and options-wise.

While there are still several HPC software vendors who have not yet extended an arm to the public cloud, many have shown sight into the future—a future where fewer environments are fully on-premises. Since HPC cloud usage is not an "all or nothing" proposition with the possibility to "burst" into the cloud for additional resources at times of peak needs, having licenses that can hop between infrastructure is critical, if not complex for both the builders of the cloud middleware and the business leaders at major HPC software companies who must retool their formerly simple models for calculating their revenue based on licensee or physical node counts.

Engineering and simulation software maker, ANSYS, is one of the larger HPC software companies that has taken the major leap to the public cloud with a new licensing approach. It has put its code into a public cloud environment. The ANSYS Enterprise Cloud takes the idea of HPC licenses for cloud in an interesting direction via what is best described as a "half-step" to full cloud models. This is not necessarily a bad thing for any parties; the infrastructure provider, the ISV, and the user. Let's take a closer look at ANSYS and Amazon have partnered to provide the provisioning of the right-sized cluster and configuration for a user's workload. This is not to say that the way ANSYS managed its cloud is the only way (or the correct one) but they do show one path for ISVs with expensive, on-premises rooted codes.

As director of strategic partnerships at ANSYS, Barb Hutchings, described to *The Next Platform*, users are billed for both Amazon consumption and the ANSYS cloud licensing separately and the behind the scenes complexity of setting the cluster up for the workload is handled when the user submits the job through the ANSYS cloud gateway after also setting up a virtual private cloud (VPC) account on Amazon Web Services. At this point, the user moves out of the way and lets ANSYS manage the setup and configuration of the VPC nodes for their software, obscuring the process and doing whatever license magic they have worked on with Amazon to make the price agreeable for both users and themselves. Direct pricing data is not easy to come by, but needless to say, licenses for ANSYS are notoriously expensive, and it is likely that either way a user chooses to go (pay a local network license of $30,000 and up for ANSYS mechanical license, for instance) or run their engineering simulations in the cloud, it is not a cost-saving measure if carried out over the long haul, particularly if one adds extended AWS usage into the cost mix.

There are benefits to running in the cloud for HPC users—some that might not be as rapidly accessible for those fighting for cluster time on-site. For instance, there are many options available that might not be present with an on-site cluster, including the ability to tap into GPU computing nodes on AWS or to use auto-scaling to make sure the job powers up and down only when and as needed. And naturally, it lets engineering organizations extend their reach and free up cluster resources for larger or more critical workloads. But for current ANSYS users, the golden words here are "your license goes with you wherever you run." So, in other words, and with very little detail from ANSYS in terms of how this is managed on the back-end, an existing license can be used in the cloud, from an on-demand computing partner, and of course, inside the walls of an existing datacenter.

THE STATE OF HPC CLOUD

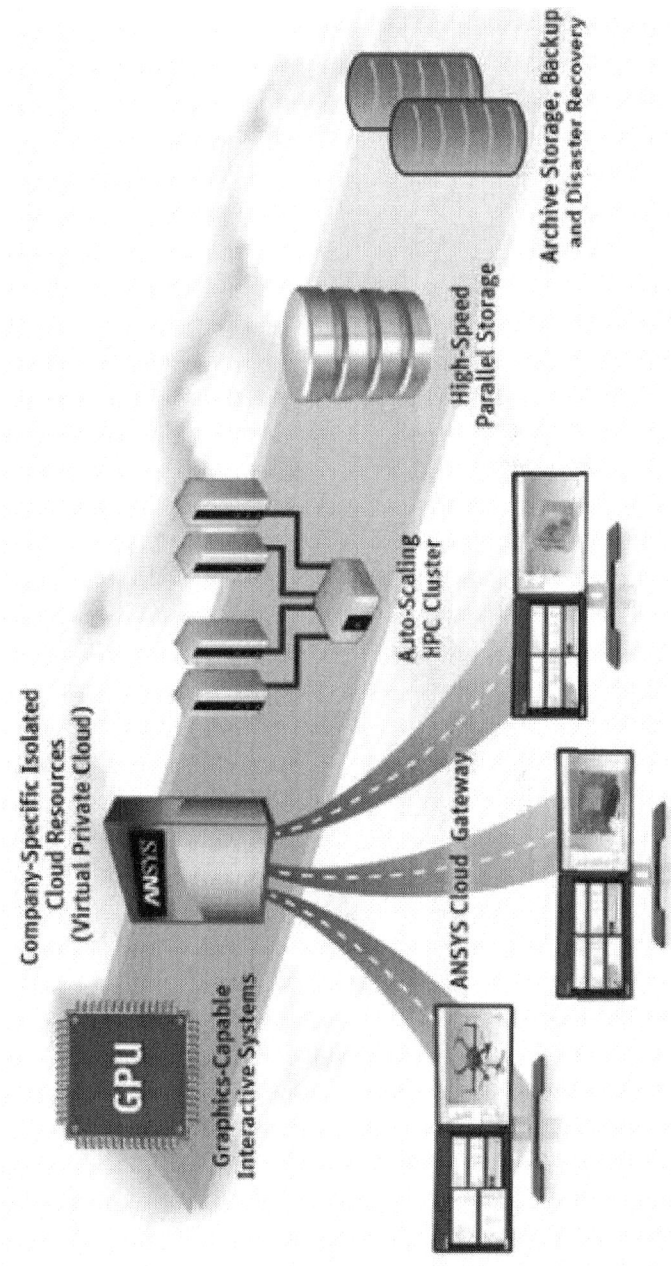

The ANSYS enterprise cloud is not seeking out that much discussed "missing middle" of industry (those who need HPC but have a difficult time on-boarding with it). Rather, those customers are being directed to HPC as a service partners that ANSYS works with through another program. This public cloud provisioning of ANSYS software is aimed at larger-scale enterprise users who rely heavily on simulation for mission-critical engineering and design tasks.

"ANSYS Enterprise Cloud is aimed at larger-scale enterprises using simulation," explains Hutchings. "With wide and deep sim deployments, these enterprises have users in multiple locations who need access to big resources, and they have users all around that need software licenses. There's been a paradigm shift from sim being deployed on every desktop to consolidating those into the datacenter for better access, collaboration, and management, and cloud is the next logical extension of that consolidation trend and the enterprise cloud we're releasing is a path to adoption if they want to move ANSYS into a cloud."

Among those large-scale users of simulation is HGST, which is one of a handful of early testers of the service. According to Steve Phillpott, chief information officer of the disk drive maker, "HGST sees the use of cloud computing as an important paradigm shift, providing increased business agility and the capacity when and where we need it. We are impressed that the ANSYS solution delivers the full end-to-end simulation process in the cloud, allowing us to maintain models, simulate and analyze results directly in our virtual private cloud (VPC) environment. Keeping everything in HGST's VPC mitigates compliance, connectivity, performance, and latency issues that are unique challenges for complex modeling and simulation workflows such as ours."

Again, ANSYS is certainly not the only HPC software company to push their software to the cloud, but they do represent how an ISV with a long history of on-premises deployments can think about the transition—and what that might ultimately mean for user flexibility and productivity.

Specialized Clouds Can Mean Specialized Licensing

While the largest public cloud providers and big name HPC software companies provide one starting point to see where HPC clouds might go, this is not the only solution, as Leo Reiter discussed in the introduction to this book.

Growing use cases for cloud have meant big headaches for purveyors of HPC software packages, which are historically incredibly expensive and are still often managed with physical dongles. Recognizing this, as well as the increased demand from users to be able to run their applications without their own clusters (or to be able to test and develop in an HPC environment), Rescale started to cultivate a base of big name ISVs with HPC packages.

"For users, the real benefit is being able to get on-demand or hourly licensing—that removes a lot of constraints on what can be accomplished. For instance, at the most basic level, there is an engineering software package that a user wants to bring their license to—that is simple through our portal. But at the highest level, with something like Siemens PLM, we have that entire suite of simulation tools for purchase on demand or hourly directly through our interface. There's an hourly price, although there is a premium because it is hourly versus annually, but it is right there and available immediately," CEO of Rescale, Joris Poort explains.

Poort's company focused on more specialized infrastructure and use cases for the cloud, including challenging machine learning and HPC codes. In this case, as with Nimbix and other specialized cloud vendors, being smaller can make a big difference for software companies hoping to capture adoption use by expanding usage models. "For ISVs, this is interesting because it is an opportunity for a new revenue stream. In the case of Siemens [who the company worked with last year], for example, the specific use cases they are targeting are for users running thousands of models in parallel at the same time. Nobody is going to buy that kind of licensing, so they've come up with a more flexible licensing model that is now open this way using this and other licensing mechanisms we are deploying."

Poort says that other major engineering simulation vendors they have partnered with, including LS-DYNA, CD-ADAPCO, and others, are also offering hourly licenses through the interface and can also expand their use cases by being more flexible with how they consider their pricing—even if it means charging a premium on that few hours since the full annual license can be prohibitively expensive for small engineering shops or for a short-term need that would otherwise necessitate a hefty license cost for what would otherwise be a spotty requirement.

ISVs are not the only ones who might benefit from expanding their users via the cloud, Poort says. Since Rescale (as well as Nimbix and others) provides a range of hardware flavors, users can see how their models perform using Nvidia Tesla GPU and Intel Xeon Phi coprocessors, and for some specialized cloud vendors, FPGAs, on the hourly license and hardware costs to evaluate what they might purchase for their future on-premises systems. "While we do offer a recommended hardware configuration for different applications, it's possible to try out different configurations, say for instance, running the job on Haswell versus Ivy Bridge, with or without InfiniBand, with the high memory options, or other specialty configurations. These are options for expert users but we do not want to place a lot of restrictions, especially since there is a lot of variation in terms of what HPC applications need."

Poort says HPC has apparently come a long way in the cloud, something that many had been expecting and others have been skeptical about. "When we first launched over four years ago, users were hesitant to try anything even related to cloud. Certainly, HPC workloads had a bad reputation on top of that, but that conversation has changed a lot—both from a performance and security standpoint. On the performance side, the way virtualization works and the way we've been able to tap into supercomputing centers has allowed us to reach similar performance to on-premises."

Poort also explains that security has evolved over the years but more important, the geographic regions that users can choose from have enhanced the sense of security—not to mention keep in step with country laws that require some work to be kept within borders. He noted that the automotive market in Japan has become a hot customer set for Rescale, but they tend to keep most work inside Japan unless there is a requirement from one of the engineering offices in the U.S. or Europe.

"We've seen a transition from users looking at Rescale as an overflow capability to them looking at this as a more permanent solution. A lot of that is because our pricing has also changed for these specialty jobs that would be hugely expensive in both hardware and software to run. We built ScaleX Enterprise for these users who want longer term capacity—these users have done the math between what they can get if they built and maintained a cluster themselves and are seeing that it can actually be cheaper to use Rescale."

It's difficult to put a statement like that into any price comparison since the one big factor—the software license costs—remain mostly unknown, as does the scale. While the hardware pricing is on par with what AWS offers for general instances (not the specialty GPU and Xeon Phi), the big cost lies in the size of the model the customer wants to run and what those licenses add to the overall price. Again, the benefit of using any of the infrastructure providers is that models can scale to new heights of complexity without adding more nodes (and thus licenses) and then spin back down when they're done. This is a compelling model but the pesky software licenses have held things back in the HPC market in particular.

In other words, on both the hardware and software front – and for both the users and the vendors–there is something to gained, which is at the heart of how politics work. Poort and the Rescale team plan to continue campaigning to keep adding more software possibilities as HPC simulation software users keep moving along infrastructure election cycles.

It has taken a number of years to get to the point where HPC in the cloud is practical—at least for some applications. While the large cloud providers have added hooks for HPC in terms of more powerful networks and processors, and others like Rescale have solved some of the required HPC software puzzles by getting ISVs with HPC code to flex their license models, there is still the tricky problem of deciding what to run in the cloud, what to save for the on-premises HPC cluster, and what might be best served by a bursting models that leverage both simultaneously. The build versus buy argument for high performance computing clusters has gathered steam lately, in part because some of the critical missing pieces both performance and software ecosystem-wise are snapping into place. We will get into that in another chapter, but the licensing costs are a central part of that build or buy equation.

Licensing When You Own The Stack

While Amazon Web Services has succeeded using its fleet of infrastructure around the world and a broad base of software partners, other companies that have had a balanced mix of both software and hardware businesses are looking at cloud software licensing differently. Microsoft did build its own cloud datacenters to support the bevy of Windows Server, Office, and other applications that are its lifeblood, but for them, the users were already there—as were the licenses. In fact, if it anything, from a user perspective, it made Microsoft products easier and more flexible to consume for users.

IBM, which has a robust systems and software business, is a different use case for how licensing can work for the ISV, the infrastructure provider, and of course, the user.

From its mainframes to the modern Power architectures, few companies have pushed investments into chip designs with the gusto IBM has over the years. The software tooling for logic and other simulations has continued to evolve, both internally via proprietary measures inside Big Blue, but they have also relied on the evolution of other ISV offerings to design new chips.

The company announced that the same software stack that they have used internally for a number of years will be extended to a new crop of chip designers using a cloud-based approach that bundles all the hardware infrastructure on the SoftLayer side along with the various collections of middleware and software they have cobbled together over the years. The goal for IBM is to be able to provide some of their software as a service to ease licensing, infrastructure management, and even support (since the operating system and other configuration details remain consistent in a cloud environment of their creation), which IBM tells us will open the door to more EDA startups.

IBM saw an influx of potential new companies rolling out of the demand for sensor-based and mobile devices and how there could be a fresh explosion in the startup chip market. This would mean fast access to EDA tools, potentially from a new crop of users who were more aligned with the startup "on demand" than the "own and maintain your own cluster" line of thinking. While IBM did not divulge exact pricing on the IBM SoftLayer based EDA cloud offering, the company says it will significantly lower the barriers to onboarding in the chip design space, particularly on the middleware and software licensing fronts.

"One thing that is big here if you look at costs for EDA startups is the ability to do hardware and software simulations. With a new generation of SoCs, then also with FPGAs, GPUs, and so forth, it is going to be increasingly important for people to simulation both the hardware and software together before they tape out their designs and build hardware that does what they want it to do," Carl Anderson, IBM Fellow and long-time Big Blue vet from the microprocessor design camp told *The Next Platform*.

Chip startups using EDA software are an excellent case study as we look at the benefits of extending cloud pricing and usage models to HPC users. For chip startups, the barriers aren't just a matter of pure cost, and as Anderson says, the hardware costs are negligible compared to the software pricing. It is also a matter of being able to scale for the more demanding segments of the EDA workflow. There are some benefits to having access to the scalability of a cloud environment, especially when it comes to some of the more expensive (computationally and licensing) elements like co-simulation of the designs to ensure the systems will work in as near of a production environment as software can fake. The logic verification end of this is where IBM is looking with its EDA cloud—and with the tuned environment and some cool tricks learned over the years in the EDA house inside IBM, the teams have been able to get a 10X boost performance-wise over other approaches to logic verification. As Anderson explained, "At IBM, we spend over 90 percent of our EDA compute cycles doing the hardware/software verification. Over the last decade we've finally been able to boot a true operating system (instead of a miniature version) on all of our mainframe and Power processors because of the amount of co-simulation we're able to do."

In terms of workload management and scheduling, the SoftLayer cloud is hooked together with IBM Platform LSF, another framework very familiar to many HPC cluster managers. As we know from a previous conversation with former Platform Computing execs (who spun off their own competitive offering to Platform LSF) a majority of large-scale users in EDA users in the space have used LSF exclusively for a number of years, a fact that might make this offering more in line with what could otherwise be missing if they tried to spin up an EDA environment on another public cloud (not to mention the challenges of getting logic simulations to run there—or talking the locked-down EDA vendor community into extending their licensing models to meet the big cloud). In short, IBM is bringing familiar tools to bear in an unfamiliar environment, at least for users who were used to running their EDA packages in-house.

What is noteworthy here is that the use model for many HPC applications in the cloud, which is bursting during times of peak need (instead of overprovisioning to meet those demands), using the IBM SoftLayer cloud might be quite difficult because all the tooling will have to be ported and consistent to seamlessly burst. Anderson says his teams recognize that is an issue and also, that this is not a fully automated path for EDA companies into the cloud. There will be some work to do to make sure codes can run on the new infrastructure and with the new tools, which means the use model is really one of full-time production clouds exclusively in IBM's cloud. Security issues might make some startups a bit jumpy, especially in a security and IP protection-centric field like EDA, but Anderson says the security of the cloud is robust and is the same that users of any of SoftLayer's customers would expect.

"For bursting in particular, it's going to take some real work for the logic simulation part of this. But for the library simulation, it should be reasonably straightforward. We have a partner, SciCAD, which is helping on the support side with this to get users quickly moving with their libraries by helping them move from their current library characterizations to the IBM one. The logic simulation though will be tricky but can be done."

In short, instead of paying single or organizational licenses, no matter how often a piece of software is used, in this use case, prices are hourly and include a bundled cost for all the infrastructure on the SoftLayer side (the hardware, VPNs, compute, storage, etc) as well as tooling licenses.

With EDA coming into the fold and a number of other HPC software areas in oil and gas, life sciences, and other examples we will examine in this book looking to do the same, the pressure is increasingly on the ISVs in high-value domains to look to ways to flex their business and license models to accelerate adoption of their wares inside more startups. After all, they could grow into tomorrow's giants and without alternatives at the beginning stages, could just as easily look to scale open source and internally developed tools that exist simply as a way around startup-crushing licensing fees.

Esoteric Software Barriers for HPC Cloud

We have looked at how a few software vendors and infrastructure providers are thinking about how their codes reach for the clouds, but having an industry perspective is also useful. If we were to consider an area where the ISVs have hefty prices and the tradition of on-premises hardware is strong, we should look no further than the oil and gas industry, with its vast seismic and other simulation and analysis needs—all within increasingly tight budgets given the downturn in petroleum prices in the past several years.

With the oil and gas industry continuing to spend on massive supercomputers, even in the wake of declining revenues, and no sign of the HPC business slowing for the oil and gas segment, one has to wonder what alternatives on the hardware and software front these companies might look to as costs (for both systems and the power required to support them) push skywards. As we are describing here, the cloud is a viable alternative to on-site processing of some HPC workloads in other industries, but oil and gas is usually not at the top of the list when it comes to segments that are offloading some or all of their critical work to public (and even hybrid) cloud providers. In some ways this is not a surprise. The problems with executing high performance computing applications in a cloud environment are well known. Latency, the transmission of large data volumes, inadequate software license models for complex simulation applications—these are but a few of the frequently cited roadblocks.

Even still, over the last few years in particular, especially as the infrastructure at the various public cloud providers has been firmed up to support HPC in the cloud (the addition of 10 Gb/sec Ethernet, more powerful Xeon processors, GPU compute nodes), a crop of new use cases has emerged. Many of these uses are in areas like life sciences and manufacturing and it is rare to hear much about the oil and gas industry's use of cloud.

This is for a few key reasons including data locality and security (oil companies are notoriously worried about data protection so others don't swoop in and drill in their locations—a fact complicated by distributed datacenters for reservoir modeling). There are more technical issues that go beyond the common security woes – but past the typical performance worries about latency.

According to Morgan Eldred, a former strategic IT projects manager at Shell and Maersk Oil, now a Gartner analyst who follows oil and gas IT infrastructure, at the top of the technical list of cloud barriers for oil and gas, is the need to access mission-critical applications. Even though companies like Schlumberger are offering a high-end and newly architected cloud-based offerings that rework both the way the application runs in the new environment as well as the licensing model, this is still not an ISV trend. Most of the existing software vendors in this area still use physical dongles to manage license use, after all, says Eldred. For that matter, the same is true in other sectors, including manufacturing where it is only just recently that high-end engineering simulation capabilities from companies like ANSYS are available via a cloud model.

As he told *The Next Platform in early 2016,* one of the biggest challenges for running large-scale oil and gas simulations in the cloud—one that trumps the performance barriers of running a node-to-node communication sensitive workload in a remote environment—is that the software itself is not primed for new architectures. "There are multiple applications in oil and gas running on HPC systems; from deep processing of data, to 3D visualizations of models, to simulations of deep earth events that are massive in scale. For those big simulations, even if you throw huge processing power, it always comes down to dependency on the way that application has been programmed."

For many of the companies that might look to cloud for their large-scale simulations, one of the barriers is simply that to reduce data movement delays and costs to and from the cloud, the only proposition is to go "full cloud" and keep data there, using the cloud as a terminal. That is a scary prospect for oil and gas companies, especially since, as Eldred notes, "for certain firms, especially in Russia, the Middle East and elsewhere, that data is the lifeblood of the organization. What happens in a reservoir under the ground does not follow national borders, so if another company gets the data, it becomes a big issue."

Eldred says that there have been major shifts toward the cloud for large oil and gas simulations at a few of the major companies. While he was unable to name the oil giants involved, he said that while this was not an enterprise-wide shift into the public or even hybrid cloud, it was proving valuable for smaller pockets of engineers and researchers for spotty project demands. The large supercomputers these companies have are often occupied with mission-critical simulations, some of which might be able to consume all of

"There is no way around the applications problem without re-architecting code if it was developed internally. The scientists who run simulations are working with mostly legacy architected simulations. Learning to run these things is not a simple undertaking—there is a lot of scripting, batch processing, and complexity."

the machine. Having on-demand access to compute resources is useful in such a case in terms of cost as well as users are able to spin up and automatically scale down their compute without moving it into queue to run on a massive power-hungry oil and gas supercomputer.

While the "spotty demand" use case for moving some workloads into a cloud environment is nothing revolutionary since it is really the primary way HPC users are interacting with public cloud resources, it is a small but important step, according to Eldred. He says that another major leap comes from the companies that are finally rearchitecting their applications for better performance under the weight of virtualization and latency as well as updating their license models to fit these users.

At the end of the day, the cloud is proving to be a rich well for compute to back computationally-intensive simulation tasks for individual research groups within a big oil and gas company, but the outlook for clouds as a high value paradigm for big companies to run full-scale simulations is not favorable, even with all the firming up of the cloud infrastructure, applications, and costs. "The human element, as in so many other industries is the real barrier," Eldred concludes. "The IP is simply too valuable, and the 'all or nothing' approach to avoid having to move data around" looms too large for big oil to process.

For oil and gas, the requirements are complex outside of just technical capability. The software and glue to hold together complex packages is critical. But for some other industries, one of the most important elements for HPC clouds, assuming the software is available, is pure performance. After all, isn't that what "high performance computing" is about, whether it is on your own infrastructure or someone else's?

Accelerators and HPC Cloud Performance

We will talk a bit later about how the major cloud providers are tackling HPC workloads with high-end CPUs, GPUs, 56 Gb/sec InfiniBand and 10 Gb/sec Ethernet solutions. Part of the reason this is important for all cloud vendors is because these environments allow users to test these environments before adding heterogeneity into their own datacenter or applications. Of course, it also helps to add a GPU boost to workloads running on the cloud, even if there will be a latency penalty to cloud use for the foreseeable future. This latency issue is not a deal killer, of course, as we will see later in the book.

Allowing users with HPC applications to spin up an accelerated cluster and power it back down later, paying only for what they use, can be a real driver for innovation. This specialization of infrastructure, which was described in the introduction, is what will make HPC clouds really take off, especially when the codes are locked in and ready to use.

To examine this, consider HPC cloud startup Nimbix, which got its start back in 2010, when the term "cloud computing" was still laden with peril and mystery for many users in enterprise and high performance computing, At the time, there were only a handful of small companies catering to the needs of high performance computing applications and those that existed were developing clever middleware to hook into AWS infrastructure. There were a few companies offering true "HPC as a service" (distinct datacenters designed to fit such workloads that could be accessed via a web interface or APIs) but many of those have gone relatively quiet over the last couple of years.

When Nimbix got its start, the possibility of running HPC workloads in the cloud was the subject of great debate in the academic-dominated scientific computing realm. As mentioned above, concerns about latency in the performance-conscious realm of these applications loomed large, as did the more general concerns about the cost of moving data, the remote hardware capability for running demanding jobs, and the availability of notoriously expensive licenses from HPC ISVs.

While Amazon and its competitors plugged away at the licensing problem, they were still missing the hardware and middleware specialization needed to make HPC in the cloud truly possible, even those AWS tried early on to address this by adding 10 Gb/sec Ethernet and multicore CPU options – and later, lower-end Nvidia Tesla M2050 and then GRID GPUs). In those early days, this difficulty is what fueled the rise of other HPC cloud startups like Cycle Computing, which made running complex jobs on AWS more seamless—but the other way to tackle the problem was simply to build both the hardware and software and wrap it neatly in a cloud operating system that could orchestrate HPC workflows with those needs in mind.

This is the approach Nimbix took and it quickly set about adding unique hardware in addition to building its JARVICE cloud operating system and orchestration layer, which is not entirely unlike OpenStack. The custom-built JARVICE platform sits on top of Linux to allow it run on the heterogeneous collection of hardware that sits in a distributed set of datacenters in the Dallas metro area (with more planned soon, including in Europe and Asia). This software manages the clusters and workflows, assigns resources, and manages the containers that power user applications. In short, it gave heterogeneous cluster capabilities on-demand, something that opened the door for HPC exploration and real world application use cases early on.

Leo Reiter, CTO at Nimbix says, its typical HPC cloud users fall into two categories. There are the bread and butter simulation users with many solvers and applications in the library of scientific and technical computing applications Nimbix has license agreements with. For these users, they provide the data and performance parameters and the system orchestrates the workflows using JARVICE and its container approach to application delivery. Counted in this group are other users with high performance data analysis or machine learning needs. On the other end are its developer users, who can use Nimbix as a PaaS to deliver their own workflows or applications and stick those in the public or private catalog. Of course, to do all of this with high performance and scalability means the Nimbix folks had to give some serious thought to hardware infrastructure.

Nimbix is also showing how users can experiment with different architectures without making big datacenter investments by providing Xilinx FPGAs—something it has done in its cloud since 2010 for both researchers and the Xilinx development team. Like the other large and specialized cloud players, they also have a wide range of Nvidia GPUs—from the low end, Maxwell-based parts for the Titan X (for machine learning training) to the new M40 processors for deep learning all the way up to the Nvidia Tesla K80 cards for those with high performance simulations and analytics. Much of the processor environment consists of 16-core Haswell Xeon parts, from which they can create secure, fractional nodes from as needed (making a 16-core part socket look like a 4-core node with the necessary memory apportionment, etc.). Nimbix also use InfiniBand networking for all nodes and for the storage system. So far, its cloud compares only to some elements Microsoft has integrated (they now have some K80s and InifiniBand capabilities) but overall, Reiter says, Nimbix is succeeding because no other cloud provider is making the hardware investments to quite the same degree. He points to the fact that there are GPUs on AWS, but the Tesla GRID parts aren't meaty enough to handle the seismic, bioinformatics, engineering, and other HPC oriented workflows—and even for deep learning training these are insufficient to their users.

What is interesting here is that just as companies that have specialized in HPC hardware are finding their gear is a good fit for deep learning training and broader machine learning applications, so too is Nimbix finding a potential new path. It has managed to carve out a niche in supercomputing and a few other areas, but so far, there aren't a lot of robust, tuned high performance hardware options as a service that fit the machine learning bill. We noted that Nervana Systems (recently acquired by Intel) is doing this, and there are a few others who are offering deep learning as a service, but a company that HPC users might know might be very well positioned as deep learning and HPC merge in some application areas and require a remote sandbox—or eventual production environment.

Reiter says Nimbix is seeing more interest in deep learning and machine learning and have added robustness to their software stack with hooks for TensorFlow, Torch, and other frameworks. Since it already has the heterogeneous hardware on site and a proven business model, we could see Nimbix move from a quiet company from the research regions of HPC to push into greater visibility via a new crop of machine learning applications and end users.

Again, Nimbix is not the only company to see that specialized accelerators can add to the cloud bottom line. The public cloud is precisely as conservative and innovative as the enterprise customers that make use of it. Clouds are a great way for many organizations to share a new hardware technology and see how it pans out running real applications, whether designed by third parties or created in-house. While GPU accelerators have found their place in the upper reaches of the HPC and hyperscale communities – doing modeling and simulation with the former and training deep learning algorithms at the latter – it is fair to say that GPU availability and adoption on public clouds is still in a nascent stage for a number of reasons.

That said, there are a number of public cloud vendors who offer GPU acceleration for a portion of their compute infrastructure, and the availability of this hybrid CPU-GPU capability is an important resource for customers who want to move from dabbling to production for certain kinds of workloads. And, we think that the adoption of GPUs on clouds could rise as software makers figure out their cloud pricing strategies (as must be done in the traditional supercomputing market) and as companies adopt an open source stack that doesn't require licensing at all (as can be done with many deep learning stacks).

It is just a matter of time, and timing, and oddly enough, the ability to run virtual desktop infrastructure (VDI) from public clouds with virtual CPU and GPU slices could get enough capacity out there on the cloud to get customers chasing it. Moreover, IBM's SoftLayer cloud continues to forge ahead with GPU-accelerated bare metal servers, which it first started delivering back in 2012, and has recently announced it is offering customers to ability to fire up Nvidia's latest dual-GPU Tesla K80 coprocessors on its bare metal instances, not long before Amazon Web Services announced the same.

It has taken the better part of a decade for even a respectable portion of the aggregate compute in the world to be put out onto the public cloud, so we should not expect for the GPU portion of compute to be particularly large right now. Nvidia first commercialized GPU computing on its video cards back in 2008, and over the ensuing eight years has rolled out a succession of specially tuned GPU compute engines with features designed specifically for accelerating simulation and modeling workloads, both in the traditional HPC and financial services industries. That HPC and Cloud business, had $279 million in revenues for Nvidia's fiscal 2015 year ended in January, as we reported in our detailed financial analysis of Nvidia back in May, and the business was growing at 53 percent year-on-year. Through fiscal 2015, Nvidia has shipped 576 million CUDA-capable GPUs and 450,000 Tesla GPU accelerator cards for servers.

You might presume that for workloads that only require single precision floating point math – or even FP16 mixed precision or 16-bit math as many deep learning algorithms can get by with – sales of GeForce cards like the Titan X cards aimed at deep learning are in these HPC and Cloud revenue figures. But they are not. Those HPC and Cloud revenues are for Tesla-only co-processors.

"CEOs and more importantly IT directors want datacenter, enterprise-class solutions," Ian Buck, vice president of accelerated computing at Nvidia, told *The Next Platform in early 2016*. "While some researchers might deploy Titan X at small scale, once you scale up with a sizable investment, you need features like ECC, system management, maintenance and support, an accelerator that has been fully qualified for 24×7 datacenter usage, and a system provider that will stand by the solution. The Tesla K40 is the most popular GPU for deep learning in the datacenter, as it offers the largest single precision individual GPU performance which gives the quickest training time for a network." Now, with the K80 available in the cloud, one can expect to see more GPU accelerated clouds for both high performance computing and, as we will describe later, machine learning.

When we talk about GPUs in the cloud, we only talk about Nvidia since there are not AMD or other GPUs (that we are aware of, anyway) on public clouds. At the moment, Nvidia identifies six cloud providers that provide cloud-based GPU capacity or hosted GPU capacity. (The former is available on demand at hourly rates, while the latter is for longer-term hosting engagements.) Amazon Web Services was the first to offer GPUs on demand among the big public clouds, back in November 2010, when it put Tesla M2050, using the "Fermi" GPUs from Nvidia, on its CG1 compute instances, which sported "Nehalem" Xeon X5570 processors from Intel and 10 Gb/sec Ethernet networking to link nodes together. Those Tesla M2050s provided 515 gigaflops of double precision floating point oomph across their 448 CUDA cores, and each node had two of them; AWS allowed customers to glue up to eight nodes into a baby cluster with 8.24 teraflops aggregate and if they needed more than that, they had to call.

Three years later, AWS launched its G2 instance types, which use Nvidia's GRID K520 GPUs, which are useful for both compute and visualization work. These server nodes, as it turned out, had four K520 cards and used Intel's "Sandy Bridge" Xeon E5 processors. In April 2015, AWS expanded the G2 instance so the whole server and all four K520s could be deployed as a single instance. These K520s are really aimed at single precision workloads and does not support error correction on the GDDR5 memory on each card. So it is suitable for seismic analysis, genomics, signal processing, video encoding, and deep learning algorithms, but not the heavy duty HPC simulations that model physical, chemical, and cosmological processes and generally use double precision math. In any event, the latest G2 instances have up to four GPUs across two cards in the server, each with 1,536 CUDA cores and 4 GB of frame buffer memory to run applications; Nvidia does not provide floating point ratings on the GRID devices, but the cores run at 800 MHz, a little faster than on the Tesla K10 that it most resembles, and that means the four GPUs should weigh in at around 9.8 teraflops at single precision.

In September 2016, AWS finally got serious about HPC on the cloud with the preview of its new P2 instances. The P2 instances are based on a custom "Broadwell" Xeon E5 v4 processor that AWS commissioned Intel to build that has 16 cores and that runs at 2.7 GHz. Each of the P2 servers has two of these Xeon processors and eight of Nvidia's Tesla K80 accelerators. If you look at the details from AWS, you might get the impression that it has put 16 of the Tesla cards in this server, but AWS is counting the individual "Kepler" family GK210B GPUs and their dedicated 12 GB GDDR5 memory chunks individually. The K80 has two GPUs, each with its own frame buffers. If would be cool if AWS actually put 16 Tesla K80s in a server – and some vendors are doing this to create extremely beefy compute nodes for deep learning and simulation – but this is not the case.

Each Tesla K80 has a total of 4,992 CUDA cores running at a base speed of 560 MHz with a GPUBoost speed of 875 MHz, and delivers 240 GB/sec of bandwidth between the GK210B and its 12 GB of GDDR5 memory. With the clock speeds cranked on all cores (which is possible if the server can take eight cards jamming at 300 watts each, as the custom AWS system must surely be able to do), each card can deliver a peak 8.74 teraflops of floating point math crunching at single precision and a third that, or 2.91 teraflops, at double precision.

The other vendors that Nvidia cites as having GPUs either on demand or hosted include Nimbix, Peer1 Hosting, Penguin Computing, Rapid Switch, and SoftLayer. Amazon offers the G2 instances in North America, Europe, and Asia and so does SoftLayer. The other players are in North America or Europe and Peer 1 does both, at least as far as the survey done by Nvidia says. We also happen to known that Rackspace Hosting offers GPUs to gaming and other customers who use its hosted servers (rather than on-demand clouds), and they are not on Nvidia's list. Google Cloud Platform does not have GPU accelerators available to cloud customers, but certainly uses GPUs to accelerate their own workloads. (Google is rumored to have over 8,000 GPUs in its stack, and it probably has well north of 1 million servers overall.) Microsoft previewed its N Series VMs on the Azure public cloud back in October 2015, based on pairing Intel Xeons with Tesla K80s. These are still not generally available as far as we know.

AWS has lots of HPC customers – the exact number is not known – but has not talked specifically about how many and to what extent that they are using its virtual clusters to run simulations, models, and other applications. The company did say when it announced the G2 instances a year and a half ago that the CG1 instances were still popular.

Marc Jones, the CTO at SoftLayer, spoke to *The Next Platform* as that cloud was rolling out support for Nvidia's latest Tesla K80 accelerators onto its bare metal cloud to give us a better sense of what is happening with GPUs on the cloud for HPC-style workloads. SoftLayer has been providing GPU-accelerated systems since April 2012, when it launched Xeon server nodes with one or two Tesla M2090 cards from the Fermi generation as an on-demand service. The company has rolled out different generations of Tesla co-processors since that time, and currently offers Tesla K10 cards (aimed at single precision) and GRID K2 cards. Neither of these cards support advanced features in the Tesla line, such as dynamic parallelism and Hyper-Q, which significantly boost the performance of certain workloads, and neither has as high double precision floating point performance as the Tesla K20, K40, and K80 units.

The bare metal servers supporting Tesla K80s will initially be available in SoftLayer's Dallas, Texas datacenter and will eventually be available throughout the 27 datacenters that the IBM cloud unit will be operating. Jones can't be specific about how many servers SoftLayer has as part of its infrastructure any more, but just as IBM was acquiring it the total number was 120,000 servers (all made by Supermicro) and the expectation was to have doubled that by the end of 2014. This did not happen, but Jones did say that by the end of this year SoftLayer will be running 46 datacenters (including those being moved over from IBM's hosting operations) and will nearly double its datacenter floor space. Our back of the envelope math says that SoftLayer would have close to 200,000 servers by the end of 2015 and lots more space to expand. We also suspect that only a small percentage of them have GPU accelerators.

While most cloud providers talk about having infrastructure on demand, for add-ons like GPU or even for anything exotic such as needing to fire up more than a few hundred nodes at the same time, you actually have to call first. SoftLayer has some nodes with Tesla K80s installed, and will roll them out worldwide, but it is really wanting to engage with customers to figure out the demand and build this to order.

To date, SoftLayer has had hundreds of customers running applications on its GPU-accelerated systems, says Jones, and it already has dozens using the Tesla K80s even as they are just being announced this week. One is the machine learning program at New York University and another is MapD, which launched a commercial-grade version of its GPU-accelerated database in March 2016.

For most cloudy GPU customers, a typical virtual cluster is somewhere between three and ten nodes, with one of two GPU cards per machine. This size of cluster has been pretty consistent over the three years that SoftLayer has been peddling virtual *ceepie-geepie* iron. Given SoftLayer's bare metal cloud and it popularity among the oil and gas industry, it is no surprise that these were the early adopters of running GPU workloads on demand. The gaming industry and video rendering and transcoding applications are also steady users of the hybrid systems on the SoftLayer cloud. In the Dallas datacenter, the GPU nodes can be linked with InfiniBand networking and have "Haswell" Xeon E5 processors from

Intel, which have a certain amount of their own integer and floating point kick. The nodes can run Windows or Linux (just like those offered by AWS) and they come with up to 512 GB of memory and flash SSDs in 800 GB, 960 GB, and 1.2 TB capacities.

"You can really trick out one of these servers," says Jones with a certain amount of pride.

The servers that the Tesla K80 GPUs can plug into can be equipped with a pair of six-core Xeon E5-2620, ten-core E5-2650, or twelve-core E5-2690 processors. Each Tesla K80 card costs $500 per month to rent, and depending on the model, a configured system ranges in price from $1,359 to $1,529 per month with a single K80 card. Loaded up with 256 GB of memory, the top-end processors, and two K80s, you are looking at $2,409 per month. The Tesla K80 card costs $5,000 list price, so SoftLayer can get its bait back at list price in ten months on the card alone, and we are pretty sure it can get a volume discount from Nvidia, so the return on investment is better than that. And, as AWS clearly demonstrates, servers and GPUs can stay in the field for many years and still make money for a public cloud provider.

This still comes down to experimentation. "In a lot of cases, customers want to try GPUs for HPC, but they don't want to make the initial capital investment," says Jones, echoing the main reason the public cloud is in general popular. "Sometimes they will try it virtualized with GPUs, and then they try it with bare metal, which gives them better and more consistent performance. In many cases, such as in the oil and gas industry, it may not be a 24x7x365 workload, but they may have a job running for six or eight months and they want to max that out. That said, we do have customers with a certain degree of steady state who keep their GPU workloads going. These are usually data analytics workloads, not simulations."

There is not, by the way, a lot of bursting of workloads from HPC centers to the SoftLayer cloud, something that people have talked about doing for a lot of years in the HPC community.

One of the tough things for any public cloud provider to try to figure out as they look to add accelerators to their compute farms is precisely what co-processors to add. Nvidia has several flavors of GPU cards, and then there are also FPGAs from Altera and Xilinx to consider, too. They have to make their bets and do the best they can. AWS is leveraging the infrastructure it needs for a VDI service as GPU accelerated compute, but some of the top features of the Tesla family are not in these cards. SoftLayer is going full-bore with the Tesla K80s, but it should probably also consider using the Nvidia GeForce Titan X cards, which are now based on the "Pascal" GPUs and which cost much less than a Tesla K80. For certain workloads, this is the right card for the job, even though it does not have a Tesla brand on it. But that means splitting the base of GPUs in two.

Decisions, decisions. Some things are just tougher for clouds than for enterprises, which control their own workloads.

The Hosts with the Most (GPUs)

While we have just touched on it so far, however, we should look to what the largest public cloud has done to accelerate HPC and machine clouds. In the public cloud business, scale is everything – hyper, in fact – and having too many different kinds of compute, storage, or networking makes support more complex and investment in infrastructure more costly. So when a big public cloud like Amazon Web Services invests in a non-standard technology, that means something. In the case of Nvidia's Tesla accelerators, it means that GPU compute has gone mainstream.

In years gone by, AWS tended to hang back on some of the Intel Xeon and AMD Opteron compute on its cloud infrastructure, at least compared to the largest supercomputer centers and hyperscalers like Google and Facebook, who got the X86 server chips earlier in the product cycle. But in recent years, Amazon has been on the front end of the CPU cycles among its cloud peers, shipping "Haswell" Xeon E5 v3 processors in the the C4 instances in January 2015, about four months after Intel launched them, and in the M4 instances in June 2015, nine months after their launch. Amazon similarly added "Haswell" Xeon E7 v3 processors, which were launched in May 2015, inside of its X1 instances in May 2016. That was a year between when Intel launched and when AWS had the X1 instanced up. And a month later, Intel launched the Broadwell Xeon E7 v4 chips, and there is no way that AWS didn't know they were coming then and there is no way that if AWS wanted to be among the first to deploy the Xeon E7 v4 processors in the world (not just among cloud providers) Intel would not have been thrilled to sell them a couple of ten thousand of them.

Obviously, AWS can't change all instance types to the latest CPUs and now GPUs instantaneously; it has to get three or four years out of each machine it installs and it has to ramp up installations along with its compute suppliers–and at aggressive pricing that preserves its margins.

AWS took issue with our interpretation of all this, pointing out that it is ahead of other cloud providers. But that was not our point. The hyperscalers and HPC shops pay a premium to get the latest chips *often ahead of their official launch* and get them installed *as soon as possible*, and the big public cloud builders, including AWS, do not do this as far as we know, and for sound economic reasons.

Here is the more important point. With the new P2 instances on the EC2 compute facility, AWS is definitely putting mainstream CPU and GPU parts into the field that can run a variety of applications, including traditional simulation and modeling workloads typical in the HPC market as well as the training of neural networks in deep learning and GPU-accelerated databases.

The P2 instances launched in September 2016 are based on a custom "Broadwell" Xeon E5 v4 chips, as we pointed out already. Again, to our point, Intel actually started shipping early Broadwell Xeon E5 v4 processors to HPC and hyperscale customers at the end of 2015 (we think in September or October), and the official launch of the chips was in March 2016, but the P2s are coming out in September 2016. AWS could have launched these in March concurrent with the Broadwell announcement, since the Tesla K80s themselves debuted in November 2014. And if AWS was really on the front end of technology, the P2 instances would have been based on Broadwell Xeons plus "Pascal" Tesla P100s, and if it wanted to stay on the leading edge, sometime in the second half of next year there would be a P3 instance with "Skylake" Xeon E5 v5 chips married to "Volta" Tesla accelerators. AWS might be installing Broadwell processors ahead of its cloud peers–the Xeon E5-2686 v4 chip was also added to the fattest M4 instance last week, the m4.16xlarge instance–but this is not exactly at the front of the Xeon or Tesla lines.

Being able to support both SP and DP math is key for all HPC cloud providers because some workloads really require that extra precision. AWS cannot build some clusters aimed at deep learning based on the "Maxwell" M4 and M40 accelerators that came out in November 2015 or the new "Pascal" P4 and P40 units that came out earlier this month because, despite all of the noise, deep learning has not gone mainstream among the enterprise customers who use the AWS cloud – although it most certainly has within the Amazon retail business itself and among the hyperscalers like Facebook that have widely deployed the M40 accelerators for this purpose. Given its desire to buy the cheapest powerful compute it can get, the cost of the flops on a Pascal P100 card with NVLink that came out in April this year are a little too rich and rare for AWS at this time, and what we hear is that while the PCI-Express variants of the Tesla P100 that came out in June offer substantially better bang for the buck than the Tesla K80s at list price, volumes are still ramping for all P100s.

Perhaps more importantly, the PCI-Express versions of the P100s have either 12 GB or 16 GB of HBM memory per PCI slot (and per GPU), but the double-packed Tesla K80 can get 24 GB of GDDR5 memory in the same space. The K80 still has a density advantage, and we figure AWS is getting a great price on these K80s, too. If AWS is getting a 30 percent discount off the K80's street price, the SP flops will be 30 percent cheaper on the K80 than on the PCI-Express variant of the P100 and the DP flops will be about the same price. If AWS is being more aggressive in its pricing, it can make the K80s an even better price/performer. The cheaper PCI-Express P100 card, at 540 GB/sec per slot, doesn't have that much more bandwidth than the K10, at 480 GB/sec across two GPUs in a slot.

By choosing the Tesla K80s, which are the workhorse GPU accelerators in the Nvidia line, AWS can cover the most bases and crank up its volume purchases from Nvidia. As more customers with different workloads come to the cloud to run their models, simulations, neural nets, and databases, AWS will be able to diversify its fleet of GPU accelerators to better match the needs of the workloads, and will also enable customers to have complex workflows that mix and match different GPUs across those workflows. This is just the beginning of Nvidia's assault on an addressable market for GPU compute that Nvida pegged at $5 billion a year ago and which is probably larger now.

The G2 compute instances that married "Sandy Bridge" Xeon E5 processors with Nvidia's GRID K520 accelerators were not Tesla-class compute and were really intended for video streaming and encoding and decoding work as well as pumping virtual desktops out of the Amazon Cloud. They were fit for purpose, and we able to be used as compute engines for CUDA and OpenCL applications if customers could deal with the lack of error correction on the GDDR5 frame buffer memory and other features found on the Tesla accelerators.

As we pointed out last July when we said that GPUs on the cloud were still nascent, these were not even Amazon's first attempt at providing GPU compute capabilities. Way back in November 2010, when HPC on the cloud seemed poised to take off, AWS put a bunch of Tesla M2050 cards on a section of its server farm (using "Nehalem" Xeon X5570 processors) and allowed customers to glue up to eight nodes together to create an 8.24 teraflops cluster. But, lighting the fuse on HPC on the cloud was a bit tougher than expected, mostly because of the issues of licensing HPC codes on public clouds under a utility pricing model, and that is why instead of deploying Teslas with the G2 instances, it went with the GRID K520s. There was a video workload that really justified Amazon's investment, and HPC and deep learning came along for the ride. It looks like there is enough deep learning and HPC work out there to justify a true Tesla investment now for the AWS cloud, and hence the deployment of Tesla K80s in the P2 instances now.

Here is how the G2 and P2 instances compare with each other in terms of their feeds and speeds:

GPU Instance	vCPUs	RAM DDR4	GPUs	vRAM GDDR5	Peak FLOPS SP	Peak FLOPS DP	SSD Storage	Network Bandwidth	OD Cost Per Hour	RI Cost Per Hour*
p2.xlarge	4	61 GB	1	12 GB	4.37	1.46	EBS Only	High	$0.900	$0.399
p2.8xlarge	32	488 GB	8	96 GB	34.96	11.64	EBS Only	10 Gb/sec	$7.200	$3.196
p2.8xlarge	64	732 GB	16	192 GB	69.92	23.28	EBS Only	20 Gb/sec	$14.400	$6.392
g2.2xlarge	8	15 GB	1	4 GB	*2.45*	*0.10*	60 GB	High	$0.650	$0.282
g2.8xlarge	32	60 GB	4	16 GB	*9.80*	*0.41*	2 * 120 GB	10 Gb/sec	$2.600	$1.128

* Assumes all upfront payment of Reserved Instances for a standard three–year term

As you can see, the P2 instances have a lot more floating point oomph and a lot more frame buffer memory and aggregate bandwidth on that memory to make use of it. The networking on the largest instances is 20 Gb/sec, and we presume that RDMA over Converged Ethernet (RoCE) and GPUDirect, which allow for data to be passed from CPU to CPU or from GPU to GPU without going through the full CPU software stack, are enabled on the new P2 instances. Add it all up and GPU accelerated instances should run a lot faster on the P2 instances than on the G2 instances.

As the first table above shows, the cost per hour for on-demand or pre-paid reserve instances (those are for standard three-year contracts for the reserved instances) is considerably higher on the P2 instances than on the G2 instances. But look at the performance differences in the second table. We have estimated the single precision (SP) and double precision (DP) floating point performance of the GRID K520 card, and the G2 instances have either one or four of these fired up with an appropriate amount of CPU to back them.

The P2 instances deliver a lot better bang for the buck, particularly on double precision floating point work. Take a look at the cost of GPU-accelerated Linux instances on the EC2 utility for a whole year:

GPU Instance	OD Annual	RI Annual	OD Cost Per SP TFLOPS	OD Cost Per DP TFLOPS	RI Cost Per SP TFLOPS*	RI Cost Per DP TFLOPS*
p2.xlarge	$7,889	$3,498	$1,805	$5,422	$800	$2,404
p2.8xlarge	$63,115	$28,016	$1,805	$5,422	$801	$2,407
p2.8xlarge	$126,230	$56,032	$1,805	$5,422	$801	$2,407
g2.2xlarge	$5,698	$2,472	$2,326	$56,061	$1,009	$24,322
g2.8xlarge	$22,792	$9,888	$2,326	$56,061	$1,009	$24,322

* Assumes all upfront payment of Reserved Instances for a standard three-year term

We divided the annual cost for on-demand and reserved instances for the G2 and P2 instances, and obviously the cost can mount up. But buying a two-socket Xeon server with eight Tesla K80 cards is not cheap either, and neither is powering it, equipping it with software, and maintaining it.

The price that AWS is charging for both the G2 and P2 instances scales linearly with the GPU compute capacity, as you can see. For single precision floating point, the price drop per teraflops is only around 22 percent from the G2 instances to the P2 instances for single precision work, but the compute density of the node has gone up by a factor of 7.1X and the GPU memory capacity has gone up by a factor of 12X within a single node, which doesn't affect users all that much directly but does help Amazon provide GPU processing at a lower cost because it takes fewer servers and GPUs to deliver a chunk of teraflops.

The fun bit is looking at the change in pricing for double precision. It is an order of magnitude less costly to have double precision on the P2 instances than on the G2 instances.

Obviously, as the table above shows, paying three years in advance for reserved instances saves a ton of money compared to using on-demand instances.

The tougher – but necessary – comparison is to reckon what it costs to build an HPC cluster on AWS using these Tesla K80s and compare it to the cost of actually owning and operating a similar cluster in your own shop. We also want to know how GPU instances on Microsoft Azure, IBM SoftLayer, and Nimbix stack up. This is a detailed exercise we will have to save for another day, so bear with. We are also working to find out how many of these P2 instances can be clustered to see what kind of virtual hybrid supercomputer can be built for long-term jobs.

The P2 instances require 64-bit, HVM-style Amazon Machine Images (AMIs) that are backed by its Elastic Block Storage (EBS) service; they do not have local SSD storage like the G2 instances did. CUDA 7.5 and OpenCL 1.2 are supported on the P2 instances. The P2 instances are available today in the US East (Northern Virginia), the US West (Oregon), and the Europe (Ireland) regions as on-demand, spot, or reserved instances as well as for dedicated hosts.

In addition to the new instances, Amazon has packaged up a new Deep Learning for AMI software stack. It includes the Torch and Caffe deep learning frameworks, the MXNet deep learning library, the Theano array library, and the TensorFlow data flow graph library.

AWS, IBM Softlayer and the specialized vendors are not the only cloud vendors offering GPUs. Clearly there is enough demand for GPU acceleration for Microsoft to make a commitment to offer it on the Azure public cloud, since that is what the company did this week at its AzureCon conference.

The details are a bit thin about Microsoft's GPU plans on Azure, and it is not clear how Microsoft is integrating the Tesla K80 coprocessors, which are aimed at compute workloads, and the Tesla M60, which is aimed at visualization workloads. Both the K80 and the K60 have a pair of Nvidia GPUs on each card and are aimed at rack and tower machines. It is interesting to note that Microsoft did not choose the Tesla M6 option for the visualization workloads, which puts one "Maxwell" class GPU in a MXM mobile form factor that might have fit better into the existing Open Cloud Server infrastructure that Microsoft deploys in its datacenters. The Open Cloud Servers have a 12U high custom chassis that fits two dozen half-width two-socket Xeon E5 servers into this enclosure. Each server node has a mezzanine card that has enough room to put a single FPGA accelerator on it, as Microsoft has done for some machine learning algorithm training and network acceleration, and we would guess that the Tesla M60 could be worked to fit in there. But a Tesla K80 or Tesla K60 could not be easily plugged into this node.

If we had to guess – and we have to because Microsoft is not yet providing details about how it is integrating the Nvidia GPUs into its infrastructure but we are tracking it down – we think Microsoft is adding GPUs to its Xeon-based compute nodes by adding adjacent GPU trays that sit alongside the CPU trays in the Open Cloud Server. It is also possible that Microsoft has come up with a new server tray that puts one CPU node and one GPU accelerator on a single tray, but that would compel the company to have a different CPU node that would not necessarily be deployable for other workloads. Moreover, Microsoft might want to be able to change the ratio of CPU to GPU compute on the fly, and this could be done by means of a PCI-Express switch infrastructure. Provided the thermals and power draw works out, Microsoft could physically deploy four GPUs in a half-width tray, giving a two-to-one ratio of GPUs to CPUs in an Open Cloud Server.

Moreover, by doing it this way, Microsoft can have the same tray support Tesla K80s for compute and Tesla K60s for visualization – and perhaps even mix and match them on the same nodes to do simultaneous simulation and visualization of workloads from the Azure cloud. (Nvidia has shown off such capabilities for a few years on workstations, so why not on the clouds?)

The Tesla K80 compute accelerator is based on a pair of "Kepler" GK210 GPUs. Each of these GPUs has 2,496 cores and 12 GB of GDDR5 frame buffer memory and 240 GB/sec of memory bandwidth. These GPUs have ECC error correction on their memory – a necessary feature for compute workloads – and support a mix of single precision and double precision floating point math, unlike the Tesla K10 that is based on a pair of GK104 GPUs, which have a slightly different architecture and are aimed mostly at single-precision workloads. While many workloads use single-precision math – seismic and signal processing, video encoding and streaming, and machine learning to name a few – there are other simulation and modeling applications that require double-precision math. And that is why for public clouds, Nvidia recommends the Tesla K80s. This is another reason why Nvidia does not suggest that cloud builders use the family of GPUs based on the GRID software stack and various Kepler and Maxwell GPUs to run simulation, modeling, and machine learning workloads. By deploying Tesla K80s, the widest spectrum of workloads can be supported.

The Tesla M60 GRID coprocessors, by the way, have a pair of Maxwell-class GM204 GPUs on a card, each with 2,048 cores and 8 GB of GDDR5 memory, and the GRID 2.0 software stack adds support for the Quadro graphics drivers and the ability to virtualized the GPU and slice it up to serve many virtual CPU instances. Nvidia does not give out floating point math numbers for the GRID family of GPUs, but we presume it has a little more oomph than the Tesla K10, which is based on the prior Kepler GPUs that have 25 percent fewer CUDA cores.

Microsoft has not provided any details on when its N family of virtual machines would be generally available using the two Tesla GPU accelerators, but Jason Zander, corporate vice president in charge of Azure infrastructure at Microsoft said they would be in preview within a few months, and that Microsoft is working with software vendors to get GPU-accelerated workloads running on the Azure cloud, presumably both Linux and Windows variants. Generally availability of the N series instances will probably be early next year. Zander did say that one of the key differentiators for the N family of Azure VMs would be the use of Remote Direct Memory Access (RDMA) over the network to reduce latency between Azure nodes, and presumably using the GPUDirect features of the Nvidia GPU accelerators, too. (Microsoft does deploy InfiniBand in some of its services, but has told *The Next Platform* that with the advent of RDMA over Converged Ethernet, it was focusing more on Ethernet in Azure these days.)

It will be very interesting to see how widely deployed the GPU instances are and how they are priced. SoftLayer was mum about its pricing, but Microsoft won't be. Amazon Web Services upgraded its GPU compute capability after Microsoft launched its N Series instance preview, and we wonder when Google Compute Platform will add GPUs. Google has a fleet of GPUs that it uses internally to train its machine learning algorithms, so it knows how to integrate GPUs with its infrastructure and scale it.

Show Me the Money

To put GPU usage in the cloud in context for HPC, consider the following financial services example, which highlights all of the concerns about clouds we've discussed so far.

Financial risk modeling via backtesting analyzes a particular strategy against historical data and trends before that strategy goes live. Despite its importance to a firm's overall strategy, securing the on-premises cluster resources to run comprehensive backtesting models is not always straightforward. And for some smaller firms, the physical infrastructure needed to scale the business with sophisticated models is a cost-prohibitive capital expense. This is, according to Justin White, CTO and co-founder of Boston-based financial tech firm, Elsen, creating something of a slow revolution, putting new firms, especially those managing under $5 million, on more level competitive ground.

Even for companies with significant investments in high performance computing infrastructure in-house, there are still bottlenecks. White pointed to experiences with backtesting teams whose simulations were pushed to the back of the queue in favor of other larger-scale or more time-sensitive applications running on in-house clusters. In such a case, having rapid ability to on-board and quickly scale meant more time spent optimizing the resulting strategy. Another client White referenced wanted to run 250,000 Monte Carlo simulations at time, but only once per week. Here we have the "perfect business case" for the cloud; spotty but intensive use to replace the cost and maintenance of a cluster that might otherwise sit idle. Using cloud infrastructure backed by GPUs, it was possible for this team to meet the scale and demand needs without having a cluster sit idle six out of seven days per week. "While it's true you may spend a nice chunk of cash for that couple of hours, compared to having someone manage that in-house system the entire week, there are real cost savings there," said White. "Even though our driving force is throughput, not cost necessarily, this is another case where this shines."

Aside from that, one of the major limitations of in-house systems goes back to scale. If a cluster for these simulations would only support ten of these simulations simultaneously, there's both a time to result and overall productivity argument to be made.

"It's trivial for us to spin up a new set of instances with the code that was on the previous system; now there are no limits in theory to how many simultaneous simulations there are." These situations, where having quick access to instant scale is key, represent some of Elsen's early growing user base, which is using the startup's cloud-based backtesting paired with GPUs from those cloud providers who offer them. (It's a short list, as we have pointed out.)

GPUs are a key differentiator for the "backtesting as a service" that Elsen is pushing. And for a small company with relatively young co-founders, Elsen brings quite a bit of GPU computing and financial services experience to bear. The company's first prototype was based on GPUs for backtesting, which was something CEO and co-founder Zac Sheffer developed while building models at Credit Suisse. Along with White and a steadily growing team, Elsen began building more robust models for GPUs, even though not all calculations for backtesting can benefit from the parallelized boost. As is the case with everything simulation-driven, a lot depends on end user applications and requirements, but the GPU angle, coupled with the freedom from maintaining on-site hardware, is where Elsen hopes to put their experience into play.

In essence, the company's system allows a user to build the strategy to test against, then run that strategy against a large amount of historical data before making the decision to move that strategy into place against a series of live data. Given the rapid, near-instant scalability of the cloud and handy access to a massive well of historical financial data, the idea is that users can quickly boost the volume of variables they look at over time. The scalability of adding more nodes, the ability to more efficiently process with GPUs, and the ability to tap into more data for backtesting at once is the driver for Elsen's belief in this model for the future of backtesting at smaller funds.

"Traditionally, people may have been used to testing across a portfolio companies—but that topped out between 10 up to 500 at the high end," White told *The Next Platform*. "Since we can scale so quickly, it's irrelevant to us how many companies they want to test against. Now users can make the quick decision to look at the entire New York Stock Exchange or the entire S&P 500 index. That's been difficult before, but it all comes down to how we parallelized this system."

The system can use the GPU to consider each company to look at as a "thread" and since one can run several thousand threads simultaneously, each company can be processed or backtested in lockstep with all the other companies, which allows backtesting at great scale and with many more variables to consider in one go. "To the GPU, numbers are numbers, as long as the algorithm is not particularly path dependent, then it will shine," says White. "Because typically our users will be running against 2,000 or 5,000 companies, every single one of those companies has a timeseries of its own, which has the exact same set of calculations applied to it that is completely independent of the other timeseries around it. So as long as the algorithm is not or strategy is not path dependent, the GPU sings."

The end result, according to Elsen, are financial modeling algorithms that run 600X faster than on CPU only-based systems.

White says the "secret sauce" is how Elsen prepares and stores data. While he couldn't reveal much, he says the format Elsen stores the data in inside the Postgres database and how it handles joins between tables for discovering data are keys, but their code yields massive improvements in how they procure and pull the data. "The whole point is that people can focus on increasing and improving their strategies, instead of working on the plumbing to actually start testing their strategies."

While Elsen can also deploy on a customer's in-house private cloud, the hosted option is dominant since its pitch is far less about infrastructure than it is about software that is designed for massive parallel jobs that can handle multiple streams at once through a single API call. On the software side, a great deal of backtesting is done using tools like Excel, and one step up from that is Matlab, but in these cases, a great of the effort is spent on building strategies versus using the time to optimize and understand them. According to Sheffer, "A lot of those generalized tools don't always have the best support for parallelizing some of the actual functions. So, for example, Matlab has the distributed toolbox, which is great, but if you can't get the data to the GPU fast enough that it doesn't get you anywhere."

It's this type of bottleneck Elsen is countering. The goal is to take the entire chunk, dropping it wholesale into the system, and let users make a single API call to do something as intensive as performing a relative strength index against the entire NASDAQ listing from the last two years. Instead of them having to worry about how to implement the data, prepare it, and backtest it and then write the actual signal before getting the results, they can make one call and we take care of all the rest of it.

The core of the Elsen system is written in C with a couple of different interfaces, which are glued together with Python. The API is based on a "very webby based stack", says Sheffer. This allows Elsen to bridge the divide between hosted and private cloud environments. Postgres and JavaScript round out the software stack. While Elsen is not accelerating Postgres (not yet, anyway—this is an area the company is working on), the cloud and performance angles are setting Elsen apart, says White. There are a large number of software companies catering to backtesting, but as of yet, there is little momentum among them to offer these services with GPU acceleration in a cloud environment where the infrastructure and software sides are abstracted away.

When one thinks about financial services for cloud, the limiting factor is always performance, even though companies like Amazon Web Services have tried to correct that by adding high-end processors, 10 GB Ethernet, and other performance enhancements to suit the HPC set. Although many in-house high performance computing clusters are used for backtesting strategies, the computational demands far outweigh I/O concerns, which means the cloud performance hit is less important. As Sheffer notes: "For most users, we're looking at 100 GB to 200 GB of data. The network is seldom a bottleneck for these things as well and latency isn't crucial, either. For high frequency trading, its different, but the real target here is throughput—something we've worked hard to push."

For hedge funds, faster and more scalable processing confers the ability to run more complex models with more complex calculations, scenarios, and sensitivities. That can mean understanding certain risks better than a competitor, or finding a sustainable trading advantage. "Running more simulations increases both the quality of your results and your confidence in those results," says Havell Rodrigues, chief revenue officer at Elsen. "That can translate to faster time to market with new or refined strategies."

Underpinning Performance for HPC Clouds: Security, Compliance and Management

The exciting discussions around HPC clouds are often about new hardware. But for these workloads, the devil is in the details. Once software licenses are moved to cloud models and once the hardware is in place to accelerate simulations and scientific or technical workflows, the next set of concerns harken back to the early days of cloud in general. Security, compliance, and workflow management are the real issues. While there have been many advances in all three of those spheres, it is useful to understand how HPC centers are looking at these issues through industry-specific lenses.

When it comes to using the public cloud, few HPC market segments have a better story to tell than the life sciences sector. In this arena, the data sizes have grown exponentially as the cost to generate and acquire the relevant datasets have been pushed down, and while this has meant an increase in the amount of computational resources required, there are now far more options than ever before—both in terms of combining in-house cores with cloud clusters as well as on the software orchestration and application fronts.

Many of the widely used bioinformatics applications for research in genomics, drug discovery, and other shoots from the expanding life sciences tree are parallelizable, which makes them a more suitable fit for running in a cloud environment. And while all of the fundamental elements appear, at least from a distance, to be in place, especially since Amazon Web Services and other large-scale cloud resource providers are bolstering their enterprise appeal with far more sophisticated data management, application framework, storage, compute, and security tools, there are still some gaps. Accordingly, the life sciences and genomics markets are finding their cloud approaches to be meshed with vendors who offer domain-specific cloud services, just as many expected might happen when public cloud adoption was a mature proposition.

In addition to lacking some tailored, non-generalized compliance and security features, what life sciences companies are missing is a management system for dealing with petabytes of data and billions of objects, says lead scientist at DNAnexus, Andrew Carroll. "In addition, there are the challenges of operating at scale—it's not that difficult to do something that will work once or a hundred times, but when it comes to have the same system work hundreds of thousands or millions of times, there are a lot of random errors and other lower-level problems that turn out to be a big deal. From a bit flip or node failure, when you're running on the order of millions of jobs, this is a major issue."

DNAnexus is one of a handful of companies that are harnessing the Amazon cloud on behalf of users, providing an environment that can be spun up relatively quickly with all the right compliance and key management tools in place, as well as an environment for developers to port their code in and have it run on the most efficient machines inside Amazon EC2 for their workload demands, both in terms of the time to solution and for the cost efficiency. While the compliance story is strong, what is interesting here is how the company's end users, particularly on the genomics side, are making decisions about whether to build or buy their genomics and R&D infrastructure.

Carroll says that while many of their larger-scale users already have clusters in-house, many of their on-site workloads tend to be in bursts, which means they need to have integrated ways to push workloads out into the cloud. But what strikes him most about these on-premises cluster users is how the cloud is making their existing hardware investments more valuable. "If you look at the efficiency of a local cluster, let's say you're running at 110 percent. This is not a good thing because that means there are wait times. For companies that are afraid of this scenario, they tend to overprovision, which on the other side, outside of those bursts where there's maybe a 10,000 genome problem, the cluster might be used at 90 percent utilization. We're seeing that bursting into the cloud is the most efficient way to use that combination of local and Amazon resources."

Interestingly, Carroll also sees some notable trends among the smaller life sciences companies who have never invested in their own cluster. "With these users, they've had the benefit of not coming from that world. That means they have a lot more free bandwidth that would have otherwise gone into managing their IT and infrastructure, and now their energy is spent is on how they interact with the cloud." This means the IT-oriented people at the company can shift focus away just management of the metal to doing innovative new things on the applications, testing, and development fronts.

The other positive side of not having cluster resources on-site is that as workloads change, so too do the computational demands. For users with in-house infrastructure to contend with, it might be really good at one key application set, but that infrastructure (compute, memory, storage) is all fixed. "We are really opportunistic because we have a full buffet of choices form Amazon in terms of what processors we use, if we need a memory heavy approach, or need SSDs or more disk, for example," Carroll explains. His team at DNAnexus runs each application that users work with on small samples of node types to determine the best operating environment, factoring in the users need to hit a solution on time and within budget frameworks. If a user wants a particular processor type or configuration they have options to tweak it inside in the system, but Carroll says most go with their tried and true defaults.

While the backend cloud hardware story and the build versus buy questions are interesting, at the end of the day, what these users care about—what really makes the defining decision for them to consider DNAnexus— is the compliance, security, and application porting story. Carroll tells us that they have invested a great deal over the last few years in creating a system that can containerize (using LXC, Docker's security issues were the limiter) and port around the custom environments that ensure HIPAA and other compliance guarantees so that each machine is isolated and has a solid data providence structure so all operations can be tracked and reported. While it's true any company could go out and have its own engineers spin up EC2 clusters, when dealing with personal health data, it is no simple proposition, even though Amazon has a lot of this in place already to appeal to the life sciences set.

"It's not a matter of whether they are HIPAA compliant at Amazon because that is just compliance and secure of their machines. It has to happen at the data management level and when it's petabytes of data we're talking about, this matters even more at scale." Carroll explains that if a company wanted to create their own cloud clusters on Amazon or another provider's resources, it would take a team of skilled engineers several years to build to what DNAnexus has constructed. And even still, he says, if they were able to do so, their teams would be managing this. Going with a provider of genomics as a service like this allows the team at DNAnexus to focus on side elements that might otherwise be overlooked, including penetration testing and building new development tools to make application building and porting easier.

While the price is a sticky issue given the variability of hardware, applications, and data transfer (we did not explore this topic in depth) this is where the meat really is for users—at least when it comes to the build versus buy equation We've covered this topic a bit here in the past, but for now, it's safe to say that the domain specific high performance computing cloud is happening. All of this very naturally takes us into the next chapter, which takes all of the benefits and drawbacks of HPC clouds and pushes them into an economic model.

Chapter Three

Build Versus Buy: The Perpetual Question for HPC

Everything we have discussed so far begs the question of whether users should build and maintain their own HPC clusters or use time on any number of the cloud providers we have described. This decision is easy if the software required is not available in a cloud licensed model or if regulations do not permit data to leave the firewall, but for a vast number of HPC applications, the potential to make good use of clouds is there.

In the early days this would not have been the case. The networking capabilities and general purpose processors were fine for regular web applications, but for latency and performance-sensitive HPC, it was not even a question. Of course, as we have been spelling out here, those conditions have changed. The heterogenous, 40 Gb/sec or 56 Gb/sec InfiniBand or 10 Gb/sec Ethernet cluster with HPC software licenses tied in is a reality. (Now 100 Gb/sec InfiniBand and Ethernet are becoming normal, and 200 Gb/sec InfiniBand is on the horizon.) So how do centers weigh the cost of having in-house HPC, going full cloud, or looking to burst at peak times?

The bursting use case is the most sensible and many workflow management and middleware packages support hopping between an in-house cluster and the cloud. Private clouds have been extended across many enterprise HPC datacenters. But how does a center do the math when it is a question of full-bore one way or another? We can get some ideas from experts at scale,

> "Surprisingly, a lot of people are thinking about offboarding from the cloud and trying to figure out when the right time might be to do that," Michael told The Next Platform. "Other customers are pretty big in co-location and they are wondering if they should build their own datacenters. What we have found is that people do not have good models to understand the financials behind these decisions."

even if their HPC roots are a bit extended.

Although their needs and scale might be different than what is required for the typical HPC application owners, two engineers with expertise at calculating datacenter costs for Facebook and Google have released a model for calculating these costs into the wild to aid in the build versus buy decision-making process.

Neither Amir Michael, who was a hardware engineer at Google and then a hardware and datacenter engineer at Facebook, nor Jimmy Clidaris, distinguished engineer for datacenter and platforms infrastructure at Google, have a vested interest in trying to push companies in any particular direction when it comes to trying to answer that basic question. (Michael left Facebook in 2014 and is the founder of Coolan, which just came out of stealth mode in February 2015 and which is offering a server infrastructure analysis tool that brings machine learning to bear on system telemetry to help companies figure out what server components work best. Salesforce.com bought Coolan in July 2016.) Both Michael and Clidaris have taken the ride as their companies jumped to hyperscale, moving from co-location facilities and commercial servers to homegrown systems running in custom datacenters, but they know that will not be the answer for every company. The issue is more complex than one of scale, and that is why the two of them knocked together a total cost of ownership (TCO) model in a spreadsheet to help IT planners map out their course.

To make such a decision as to build a datacenter, use co-los, or just employ clouds means juggling hundreds of variables, and this is precisely the kind of thing that people are apt to use their gut to make a decision on. That is a method, of course, but not very scientific. Michael says that there are some general rules of thumb to start with.

The first rule is scale, and generally speaking, the larger you are, the more it makes sense to have your own infrastructure. "Speaking very generally, if you are spending hundreds of millions of dollars a year on infrastructure, it makes sense for you to start doing it yourself," says Michael, with the caveat that as soon as you start talking about this generally, there are cases where this does not hold true. "I purposefully did not provide a specific number for this because there is not one number."

Also, certain industries have their own issues. Both financial services and supercomputing centers have very specific hardware needs to support their applications, which are often not available in the cloud, and financial services and healthcare companies are very sensitive to the location of their data and that can limit their use of public clouds.

Customers have to weigh other issues before they even start plugging numbers into an infrastructure and datacenter TCO model like the one Michael and Clidaris have created. Public clouds have elasticity of capacity unlike what most companies can afford to build for themselves, and that capacity is fairly instantly available.

But, as we point out above, that capacity is also fairly general purpose and usually only available in precise configurations of compute, storage, and networking. The cloud is a general purpose platform, but only up to a certain point.

And that elasticity has its limits, too, such that most hyperscale companies cannot deploy on a public cloud, and even some large enterprises are getting to the point that they have to call up their cloud provider months ahead of time to ensure that the capacity they will need will be available when they need it. This is more of a classic hosting model than any of the public clouds want to talk about, but it is happening, says Michael. (Interestingly, the largest hyperscalers have turned around and created public clouds that will give them more elasticity for their own workloads as well as a customer base that subsidizes their IT research and development and helps cover the cost of their datacenters.) The point is, building your own infrastructure has its advantages even if you are not Google, Facebook, or Amazon, such as the continuity of the systems and the predictability of the supply of machinery that is tuned for specific applications.

The place that every company has to start is knowing their applications well. Without an assessment of the applications, how they are connected, and what resources they need to run with acceptable performance, a proper decision cannot be made about where to locate the infrastructure. Benchmarking on bare metal and virtualized servers has to be done and compared to capacity running in the cloud, and you can't skimp on that. The TCO model that Michael and Clidaris have created can't do this work, but once you have such data, you can input it into the model to figure out whether it makes sense to build a datacenter or rent co-lo capacity or use a cloud.

Michael provided *The Next Platform* for some use cases on how the datacenter TCO tool might be used. In one use case, information about power costs was pumped into the model to see what effect the cost of electricity has on datacenter costs. Hyperscalers are able to get low-cost power at 6 cents per kilowatt-hour in many cases, sometimes it is 10 cents per kilowatt-hour. So just for fun, Michael pumped in 50 cents per kilowatt hour (that's about 2.5X the residential rate in New York City) to see what affect it has on datacenter costs.

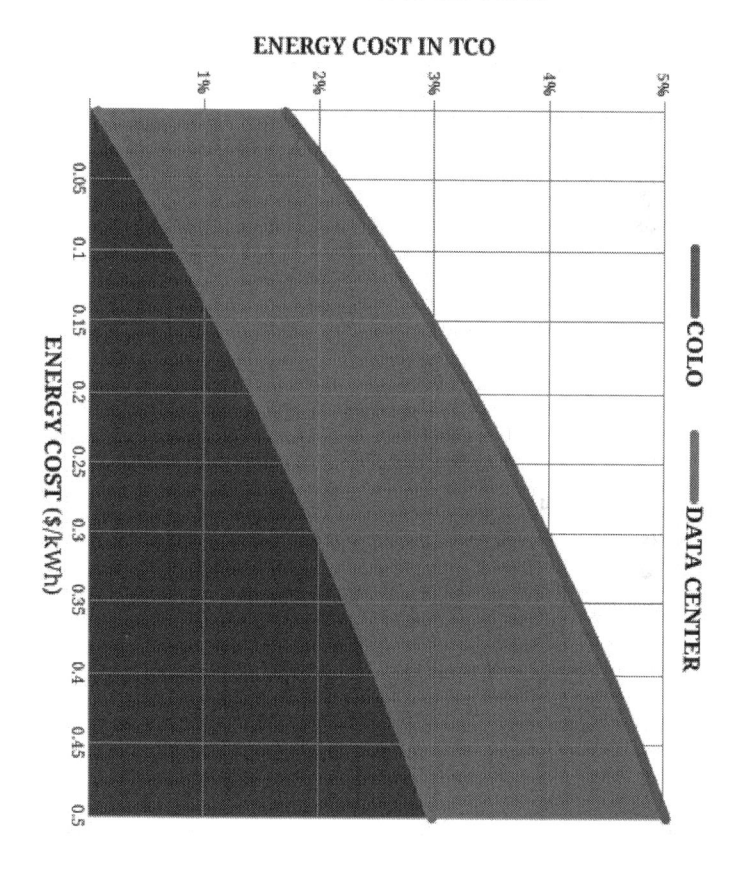

ENERGY COST IN TCO

In the example above, Michael compared a co-lo and custom datacenter housing 4,000 compute nodes and 625 storage servers, which consumed about 1.5 megawatts of juice. Because datacenters are built for the long-haul, the costs in this scenario are reckoned over an 18-year horizon. The cost of energy is higher in the co-lo than in the datacenter, but in both scenarios, the cost of energy is small compared to other factors.

"We found that the change in overall datacenter costs was almost negligible, only raising the cost by one or two points for the cost of the overall infrastructure," says Michael. "A big part of that decision is capacity, and a lot of places simply do not have tens of megawatts of excess. That is why Oregon, which has hydroelectric, and North Carolina, which has electrical infrastructure that used to support the furniture industry, are popular places to build datacenters."

We would add that while the availability of electricity capacity is the reason that hyperscalers choose such locations, they certainly negotiate hard for long-term power contracts that give them among the lowest energy costs in the world and that savings does, in fact, drop straight to the bottom line. This is one of the many cost advantages of hyperscale.

In another example, Michael pumped in a number of compute and storage servers into the TCO model and scaled them both up to see what the model would predict about costs in a private datacenter, in a co-location facility, and a public cloud (presumably Amazon Web Services). If the workload you are running is heavily compute with very little storage, it is almost always cheaper to use the cloud to run that workload. (With the obvious caveats mentioned above.) The margins that AWS and other cloud providers are making on compute are, relatively speaking, pretty slim, and that is because compute is more of a commodity than storage. If you have a workload that is heavy on storage with very little compute, then somewhere around 500 storage servers it makes sense to think about owning your own gear and using a co-location facility and at 1,000 storage servers, it makes economic sense to build your own datacenter.

As the duo point out, the real decision depends on

what your application and long-term needs look like. For HPC users, however, there is an added bit of complexity; knowing that the performance will be there in an on-demand or cloud environment.

This is useful background at extreme scale, which supercomputing certainly is, but what about the average HPC user?

Earlier in the year Rescale's CEO put forth some numbers about how his company considers HPC cloud economies. The numbers below offer a cost breakdown for on-site HPC clusters versus renting capacity and licenses, and represent the costs of a typical, middle of the road cluster for high performance computing workloads, without the highest-end processors and without any accelerators. Poort explained that this represents a midpoint for end users—some want ultra high performance, others are cost-conscious, hence the choice for this as the baseline. Naturally, once the newest Haswell processors or Infiniband or other bells and whistles are added the base costs go up, especially for the first year of the cluster.

Number of HPC Servers(Node):	100	
Number of Servers per Rack:	10	Adjust this to model power density
Number of Ports per Server:	2	
Number of Switches per Rack:	2	ToR switches, HA pair
Peak Power per Server:	2600 W	
Average Power per Server:	2200 W	
[2] Metered Power Cost per KWH:	$ 0.103	(See Note 2)
Number of Cores/HPC Server:	16	
Total Cores:	1,600	
Depreciation in Months/Rate:	36	Change to 36 for standard 3-year, 12 for accelerated 1-year
Risk Adjusted Rate:	8%	Discount rate for capital budgeting
Estimated Enterprise Discounts:	40%	
Server Ports per Rack:		20
Peak Power per Rack:		26
Number of Racks:		10
Number of Switches:		20
Design Peak Power:		260
Total Metered Power:		220
Estimated Power Cost: $		16,315.20

With the above configuration, users are looking at close to $70,000 per month just to operate a typical 100 node cluster in a physical datacenter, with around $16,000 of that cost going toward power and cooling. The figures Poort provides also include one full time engineer to manage the cluster, which he says is often not a position that disappears since most of their users, and those who have made a cloud transition, are still running many workloads in house in addition.

Here is the breakdown Poort provides of typical cluster costs:

	Price Ea	Qty	Total	
Fixed Assets				
Server, dual E5-2670 with 64GB RAM, 640GB SSD, support	$ 7,404	100	$ 740,400	Active servers in the rack
Server Maintenance at 15%/server/year over 3 year period	$ 1,111	100	$ 333,180	
Provision for Spare Servers @5% of total	$ 7,000	5	$ 35,000	Cold spares
ToR switches, 10G 48 port, 3-year support	$ 5,000	20	$ 100,000	Active pairs supporting 10-12 servers each
Aggregation Switch	$ 18,000	2	$ 36,000	HA pairs
Racks for servers, CPI TeraFrame or equivalent	$ 3,000	10	$ 30,000	With chimney cooling
PDUs, dual 208V per rack, 3VN3G60 12.6KW or equiv	$ 540	20	$ 10,800	Supporting management and monitoring
10G cabling in-rack	$ 180	200	$ 36,000	Direct attach SFP cabling, fiber
Rack and Stack 1-time deployment, per-rack	$ 1,000	10	$ 10,000	Estimated
Software Cost	$ 5,000	1	$ 5,000	Estimated
Subtotal			$ 1,331,380	
Total Fixed Assets			$ 1,331,380	
Monthly expense of above fully depreciated			$ 41,721	Monthly
OPEX - Monthly				
Data Center Metered Power	$ 0.103		$ 16,315	
Data Center base cost per peak KW	$ 150	260	$ 39,000	Multi-year contract
Assumes multi-tenant wholesale facility inclusive of cooling,				
backup power, building security and walled or caged space.				
Operations Management Non-Staff Cost per Server (nagios or equiv)	$ 50	100	$ 5,000	Per month cost
Operations and IT Management Staffing cost	$ 10,000	1	$ 10,000	One FTE @120K burdened
Subtotal (Monthly)			$ 70,315	Monthly

That is just the cluster operation, but Poort says the cost total for owning the cluster, including the support staff and other services as broken down in the charts provided, is more like $110,000 per month. The interesting part about that is that approximately $40,000 are hardware related costs, but the other almost $70,000 is operational (power, people, and related costs).

This might sound high, especially for companies where the budgets for HPC resources are broken down across divisions. For example, in some organizations, the cost for things like bandwidth are billed as part of a larger bandwidth usage monitoring mechanism. The same is true with electricity use, which is oftentimes not part of the total for an HPC cluster since the datacenter consumption is rolled in with other electricity usage. All of these funds do come from somewhere, but Poort says he realizes its easy to take issue with how large these figures are—they are simply rolling together all possible costs, even in some HPC shops pass certain large bills for their facilities to other departments.

On that note, breaking down core hour costs is a little tricky, especially since oftentimes this is calculated based on hardware costs alone. The part that is often missing from these calculations are the many other costs that are factored into the overall operational and datacenter costs as listed above. The fully burdened core hour costs at 10 cents per core hour does factor all of this in, but it's a matter of how shops calculate these things. "If you're adding just electricity and not all the datacenter costs, then you're at 5 cents per core hour, which might not sound like much a difference, but it's 25 percent more—then you add in those facility costs and other elements and it's quite a big deal," explains Poort. These are not savings that would be immediately realized, either, which is an important distinction, but over time, the difference could be quite significant.

The catch is, that 10 cents per core hour is assuming 100 percent utilization, as you can see in the chart below. "Another big misunderstanding when it comes to evaluating these costs is when one just looks at the surface at how much they are paying for a server in the cloud. The cost seems high relatively to just buying a server and plugging it in yourself, but the reality goes back to utilization—you can spin these machines up and down, you're not paying for them when you're not using them," Poort says.

	Per Node	Per Core
Monthly Cost for On-premise HPC:	$1,120.36	$70.02
Hourly cost at 100% utilization:	$1.56	$0.10
Hourly cost at 80% utilization:	$1.95	$0.12
Hourly cost at 60% utilization:	$2.59	$0.16
Monthly Rescale Cost:		
Hourly Rescale cost 100% utilization at Prepaid rate:	$0.64	$0.04
Hourly Rescale cost 80% utilization at Prepaid rate:	$0.51	$0.04

In other words, with a typical on-premises system, this is not the case and for many HPC engineering groups, the tendency is to plan for peak capacity since having the full resource push for product development is oftentimes more important than worrying about having 100% percent utilization. "A lot of companies understand that they are getting maybe 60-70% utilization, but that's a smart decision on their part because they need that peak capacity—their engineers cannot wait for simulations to run."

This goes back to Poort's argument that the ideal use case for HPC customers is to have some combination of on-premises and cloud-based resources to manage the need for peak capacity, but also to balance the costs based on existing hardware investments. He does not expect companies to go full-bore into the cloud for all of their critical HPC workloads, but does see an opportunity to expand access to both the needed diverse hardware and software tools to expand a company's existing capabilities.

As a final note, part of what we described in a previous article about Rescale was not so much about the hardware available from its collection of resources around the world (1,400 petaflops of potential peak), it was more related to the software license agreements they have managed to arrange with ISVs offering expensive, complex HPC engineering software. For a user to buy these licenses by the hour is an important (and unique) capability, which adds (rather significantly in some cases) to the prices shown above. Still, to see the hardware costs broken down from cloud vendors–and how they approach potential users is valuable insight, although the variability of HPC systems and workloads makes it difficult to set a baseline that is applicable to all.

Now that we have a sense of how the clouds evolved to meet the needs of HPC users on the hardware and software side (with help from key HPC ISVs, of course), let's take a broader look at each of the major public cloud providers' emphasis on acquiring hardware, software, and new features to reel in HPC. It should be noted that in doing so, they are also stocking their virtual shelves with the same hardware that will be in need for the new wave of machine learning applications. These require GPU acceleration, fast networking, and a bevy of libraries and tools each cloud is working to provide. In the end, what is good for HPC is good for this other growing set of users, a topic we will get to near the end of this book.

Chapter Four

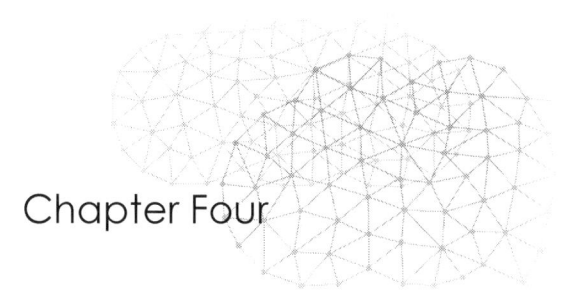

Analysis of Major Public Clouds

Letting go of infrastructure is hard, but once you do – or perhaps more precisely, once you can – picking it back up again is a whole lot harder.

This is perhaps going to be the long-term lesson that cloud computing teaches the information technology industry as it moves back in time to data processing, as it used to be called, and back towards a rental model that got IBM sued by the US government in the nascent days of computing and compelled changes in Big Blue's behavior that made it possible for others to create and sell systems against what was, technically speaking, a regulated monopoly.

It is funny to ponder what the world would look like had IBM continued to fight against the provisions of the 1956 consent decree that settled the lawsuit against it by the US Department of Justice. We may have gotten to cloud computing as we know it today a whole lot earlier, but it is safe to assume that we would not have necessarily been on a Moore's Law curve of increasing sophistication and decreasing costs that we have all benefitted from thanks to the intense competition from many platforms over the past five decades that only has Intel as its most recent champion. Digital Equipment, Novell and Compaq, Sun Microsystems, Microsoft, and the Linux collective have been champions for value in their turn, and one can make a credible argument that Amazon Web Services is a platform in its own right and is also, in its way, driving the value proposition for the cloud industry when it comes to data processing and storage.

This is an industry at a peculiar point in its history, one where the market is growing at over 50 percent and looks like it will continue to do so for some time. As John Dinsdale, chief analyst and research director at Synergy Research Group the company put it, "This is a market that is so big and is growing so rapidly that companies can be growing by 10 percent to 30 percent per year and might feel good about themselves and yet they'd still be losing market share. The big question for them is whether or not they are building a sustainable and profitable business. This can be done by focusing on specific regions or specific services, but the bulk of the market demands huge scale, a broad footprint, very deep pockets and a long-term corporate focus."

Here is how Dinsdale stacks up the cloud players:

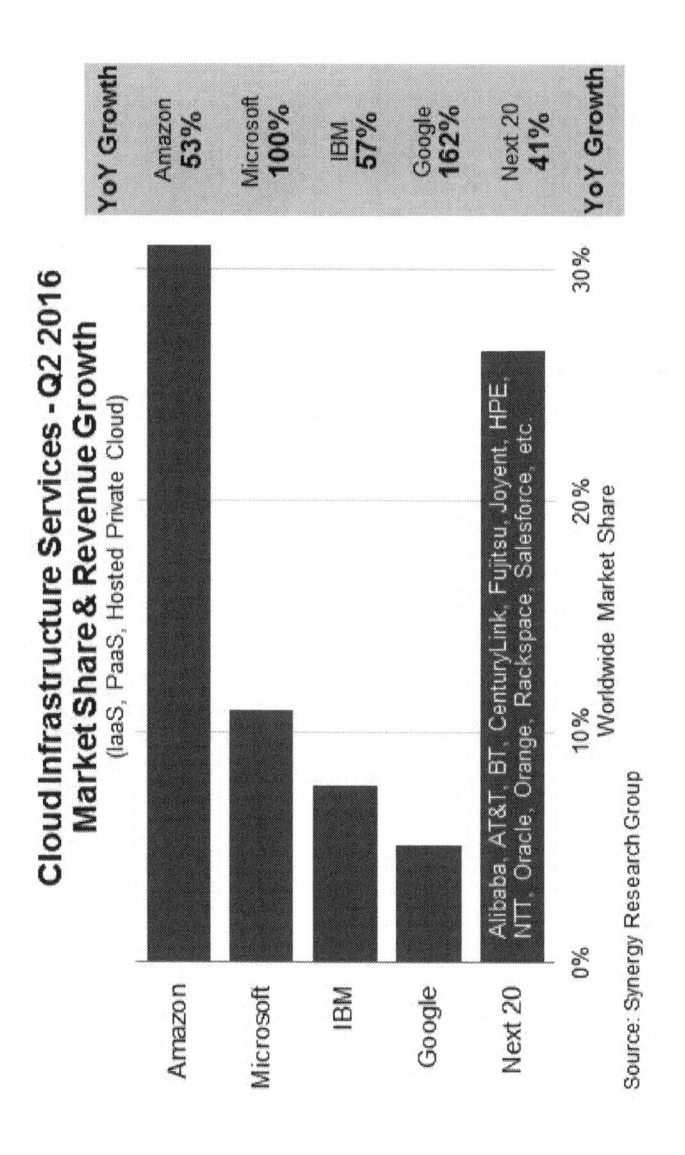

Cloud Infrastructure Services - Q2 2016 Market Share & Revenue Growth
(IaaS, PaaS, Hosted Private Cloud)

Company	YoY Growth
Amazon	53%
Microsoft	100%
IBM	57%
Google	162%
Next 20	41%

Next 20: Alibaba, AT&T, BT, CenturyLink, Fujitsu, Joyent, HPE, NTT, Oracle, Orange, Rackspace, Salesforce, etc.

Worldwide Market Share: 0%, 10%, 20%, 30%

Source: Synergy Research Group

Interestingly, the United States accounts for about half of the cloud revenues in the world, according to Synergy, as was the case for computing during the mainframe era way back when, but over time we think that as the largest cloud operators learn to go local, working with partners to build clouds that are operated by regional IT or telecom companies, the cloud footprint will actually represent a larger portion of computing inside of the emerging economies than it does inside the US and other regions that dominate the established economies. China went straight to cell phones, and there is every reason to believe that China will be enthusiastic about clouds because of the centralized command and control it offers.

Amazon Web Services

Amazon, with 31 percent share of cloud revenues in the first and second quarter, continues to dominate its peers, even though it is a pure public cloud play and is not, like Microsoft and IBM, bolstering its cloud numbers by selling infrastructure that others pay for to build their own private clouds. (Mixing acquisitions of hardware, software, and systems integration services with rentals of compute, storage, and networking capacity makes this a kind of apples to applesauce comparison, mind you. But this is the data that is out there, and this is how IT vendors talk about their cloud products so it is hard to break it down at a more atomic level.)

In the period ended in June, revenues for AWS rose by 58.2 percent to $2.89 billion and operating income rose by 135.9 percent to $718 million. Anytime an IT supplier is growing profits twice as fast as revenues, that is a win, and growing at these rates only happens at the beginning of a new market. (It is hard to believe, but cloud computing is still, even after ten years, nascent.) The growth rates for AWS are cooling a bit, but there are so many price cuts and efficiency gains that customers themselves are doing that it is not surprising at all that the curve will wiggle up and down. The thing to notice is that AWS is getting more consistent operating profits as a percentage of revenues, which suggests that it has found the magic critical mass where the business behaves more like an annuity (like IBM's mainframe business has historically done) than a new product that has to be sold feature by feature, day in and day out.

Amazon has well over 1 million customers who are adding capacity like crazy. In fact, in about two years, AWS will probably be larger than IBM's entire systems business, including sales of systems, operating systems, middleware, tech support services, and financing as well as its cloud infrastructure, which is largely based on X86 iron made by Supermicro.

THE STATE OF HPC CLOUD

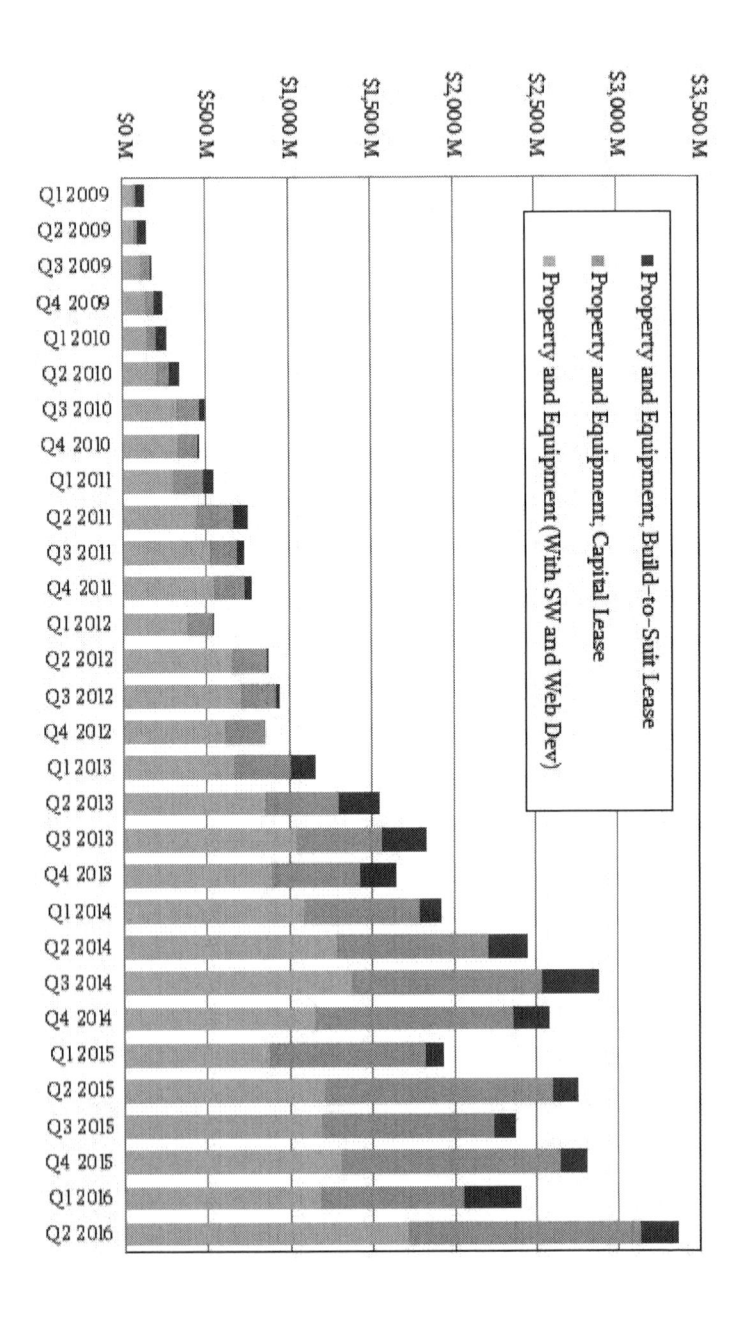

We have said it before and we will say it again: If AWS wanted to accelerate the adoption of cloud among enterprises, it could create AWS stacks for private clouds and sell them into corporate accounts. But we think AWS and parent Amazon have done the math and figured out that this would eat into profits, something that it cannot afford to do because without AWS, Amazon is essentially not a very profitable company.

Rather than turn itself into a distributed cloud, with lots of capacity in its own datacenters and perhaps an equal sized portion at large enterprises that want their own gear, Amazon is going for the cream of the crop, which means those who are creating new cloud native applications, those who are all-in with the public cloud, and those who are willing and able to build private clouds that are quasi-compatible with AWS when they want to go hybrid. All the grief and cost is on the customer in that last scenario, which is pretty smart when you are managing for profit and when you believe that, in the fullness of time, everyone will end up on a public cloud anyway, as AWS does.

THE STATE OF HPC CLOUD

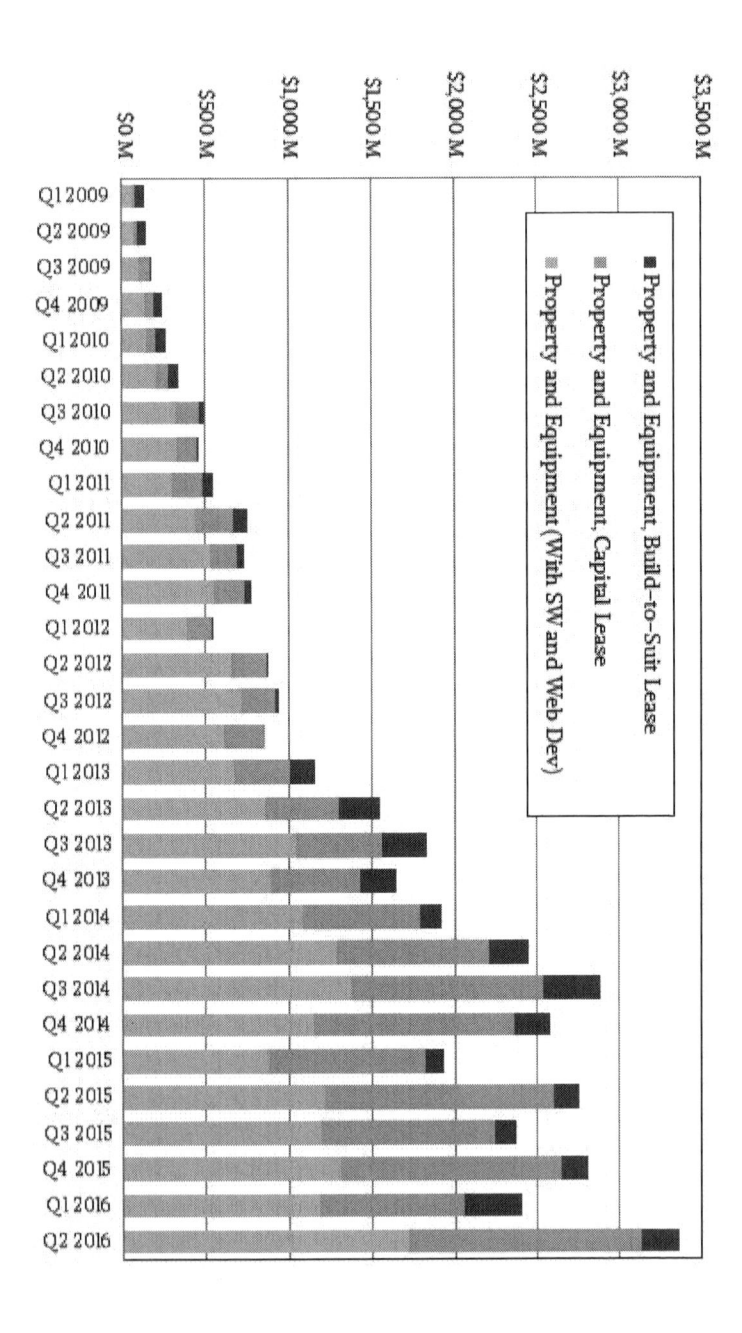

That public cloud infrastructure is enormously expensive, as you can see from the capital expenses chart above. But what seems clear is that Amazon is getting better at managing its capital, and indeed, one of the reasons why it was willing to divulge AWS numbers last year was because it has gotten better at squeezing more revenue out of its infrastructure. In the presentation above, the data for the past six quarters shows operating profits after stock-based compensation and other items are taken out, something the company started doing in the most recent quarter and backcast through the beginning of 2015. So if you are thinking AWS is less profitable than it was a few years ago, it is just that this compensation is being taken out at the group level rather than at the company level. The point is that AWS is throwing off operating profits like it is a software company, which is a neat trick for an organization that is building datacenters and all of the gear inside of it to sell infrastructure, platform, and software services on top of that.

One of the things we want to know is how large the AWS ecosystem is. In other words, what is the aggregate value of the goods and services that are sold as a platform but not including the revenue generated by the companies on the platform. Ecosystem revenues tend to be multiples of the revenues of the underlying platform revenues. The last time we did a detailed analysis of ecosystems was in 2005, when an installed base of around 19 million servers drove $365 billion in sales, with Windows comprising around 38 percent of that dough, Linux around 11 percent, and Unix about 28 percent. The multiples were anywhere from 5:1 to 8:1 comparing the underlying server platform revenues each year with the overall value of the ecosystem of hardware, software, and services sold for that platform beyond (but including) their primary vendor.

It would be interesting to separate out infrastructure services on AWS from platform services and software services from third parties to do a similar kind of analysis, and also to see at what point platform and software services will outstrip basic compute and storage services that underlie them.

For supercomputing users, Amazon was the first—and for some, including those that cater to HPC users by building bridges for high performance computing applications to the public cloud, AWS stands alone.

For workloads based on the MPI model, fast node to node communication was critical. That lack of capability in 2010 alone was a deal-killer (or at least an HPC cloud conversation killer). For those few who had the most to gain from the opportunities poised by high performance computing in the cloud, the design and engineering folks who run HPC simulations to power daily business, the performance hit was one thing—the software licensing for expensive proprietary codes wasn't being made available for cloud use. For any of these users too, the entire middleware layer—the on-ramping of complex applications with diverse workload requirements was too much to consider on top of the other limitations.

What is notable here is that over those years, Amazon Web Services listened, even to a relatively small community of end users—the HPC crowd. They added GPU instances, which was certainly appealing to some running HPC simulations in the cloud, as well as 10GbE for latency-sensitive workloads, not to mention a number of compute-intensive instances with varying degrees of oomph and memory-heavy types as well, as we have described in this book. While it's true these serve other workloads outside of HPC, the company has done a noteworthy job of making the HPC cloud connection over the years.

If AWS and its public cloud compatriots fail to attract big HPC users, it's probably not because the critical hardware is missing, or even the right middleware. It's because the culture is missing. That means the way that research HPC centers look at their workloads and where they run, all the way down to how ISVs decide how to bandy about their licensing. Because after all, if you have highly specialized HPC code you're peddling based on per-node pricing, you know damned well you don't "have" to make it available as a cloud offering if it doesn't fit your business model. Sure, your users can work with open source engineering, design, and other codes, but they don't do what yours does—and the people who work at the companies that can afford these expensive licenses have invested a great deal in the people and software partnership already.

And speaking of culture and investment, HPC sites, in commercial sectors or research, invest in hardware. Period. They have done for that for many years, thus a datacenter investment is not considered a one-time thing. It's ongoing. There is a culture of people, of datacenter ownership, of stewardship of the machines. Faced with the option of cheaper full-run in the public cloud, this isn't a question for several businesses. Even if the economics worked out, it would still be a monumental decision.

Amazon Web Services turned ten this year, and while the technology and business story has been a compelling one to watch over the years, for one segment of its user base, the real value of cloud for HPC is still an evolving story. Here's the interesting thing though. The adoption curve for HPC applications on the public cloud is far less about what Amazon (and its "competitors" in the space) does to create the right environment—and far more about what the existing HPC ecosystem does for the cloud. It's not about tooling, it's about culture.

So where *is* the heralded public cloud for HPC? Where are those long-promised full-scale production workloads humming away on Amazon infrastructure? Well, they're there, but in any cases with those "true HPC" MPI, latency-sensitive jobs, it's just sometimes– and only when centers need to avoid buying more iron.

Real HPC cloud is found in the bursting model. It's hybrid. And in that use case, at scale anyway, it is the perfect story. HPC hardware is not cheap to buy, lease, maintain, staff, and click licenses to. Assuming the licenses come along for the hybrid cloud ride (an increasing number do), seeing that peak needs require an extra 100 cores twice per month, for instance, and making the decision to simply automatically burst a workload makes good business sense. And ten years in, AWS has given enough options that the environment will not look that much different.

Because here's another benefit for HPC users on the AWS cloud. Chances are quite good, given long upgrade cycles (4 to 6 years, depending on the shop), that AWS has better hardware than you do. Yes, there's a latency hit. No, your commercial codes might not have licenses that transfer. Yes, data movement is an expensive thing for large simulation workloads. But. But…to test, develop, and run in burst mode on the latest greatest hardware on demand? How is this not the most compelling story to hit HPC in theory, if not practice, in years?

The data does not favor the view that cloud will burst into HPC budgets, however. For instance, Intersect360 Research, which publishes in-depth reports based on many high performance computing sites around the world shows an interesting flatline for cloud spending.

Table 1: Top-Level HPC Budget Distribution, N/B included

Category	2010	2011	2012	2013	2014	All Years
Hardware	38%	36%	46%	43%	45%	42%
Software	15%	15%	13%	14%	13%	14%
Facilities	11%	13%	9%	10%	10%	11%
Staffing	26%	24%	22%	21%	22%	23%
Services	7%	9%	7%	8%	7%	7%
Cloud/Utility/Outsourcing	3%	3%	2%	4%	3%	3%
Other	0%	1%	1%	1%	0%	1%

Source: Intersect360 Research, 2014

Of course, if bursting is the primary use case for many users with large HPC installations, it is fair to assume the budget room would be small since it's occasional use–and likely very inexpensive. While it will never be cost-effective to simply rent a full HPC environment equal to one hundred or more nodes for full production use in the cloud exclusively, that 3% budget room they see is enough to save an HPC site many thousands of dollars that would have gone into server over-provisioning for peak needs.

There will never be a replacement for large-scale supercomputers. While the mode of computation may change over the coming decades, outsourcing complex simulations to a cloud resource will not make economic sense, among other mismatches. But for smaller-scale high performance computing (HPC) it continues to be an attractive option for full-bore handling of HPC workloads, but more often than not, for "bursty" workloads at centers where over-provisioning HPC systems to handle peak demand times was the norm for years.

Enlightened self-interest or not, AWS has given HPC hardware vendors a run for their money—and has forced ISVs into thinking about how their licenses work in an era of "ubiquitous computing". As for the use cases for HPC cloud, they mount with each passing year, many focused on life sciences and manufacturing, as we will explore in later chapters.

Just as Amazon Web Services pioneered cloud in those early days, given its strong footing in that it already had the hardware and software infrastructure "sitting around" to sell off, it made great strides to bring its capabilities to the scientific computing community–even without a sense of how such investments would pay off. It was not an easy sell for the high performance computing folks initially (for the reasons listed above, as well as privacy and security, among others), but use case by use case, it was slowly proven out that the public cloud could be a valuable scientific computing resource—even just for occasional workloads.

There are hundreds of HPC applications that are ready to run in Amazon already, and most recently, in addition to launching K80 GPUs, the HPC teams at AWS announced Alces Flight, a service with the goal to "rapidly deliver a whole HPC cluster, ready to go and complete with job scheduler and applications. Clusters are deployed in a VPC environment for security with SSH and graphical desktop connectivity for users. Data management tools for POSIX and S3 object storage are also included."

One can expect that AWS will continue to garner favor with HPC centers as well as commercial HPC sites looking to offload at least some of their peak-time compute. Among current HPC users are the Jet Propulsion Laboratory, Pfizer, and a number of universities. AWS has most recently added their C4 instance type featuring a variant of the latest Haswell processors, one of which offers up to 36 vCPUs. They have also added "Placement Groups" for virtual clusters for latency-sensitive jobs. And over the years that AWS Marketplace has been alive, the HPC section continues to grow with 67 services and packages for the supercomputing set.

While other infrastructure providers, including Microsoft Azure, Google Cloud Platform, and IBM SoftLayer have also extended an arm for HPC end users, the marketplace approach AWS offers was the first to hook HPC end users—and it continuously focuses on this narrow, but important, subset of compute consumers. The question we've been poking at off and on over the years is how important the HPC market is for AWS overall. It has never been simple to get a sense of how many applications of this nature run, but if the best estimates are correct, it's a relatively small subset of applications. Intersect360 Research, for instance, which focuses on the HPC market, found that cloud spends account for only around 3 percent of the budget allocations at HPC sites worldwide with fluctuations year to year–and very little momentum upward.

AWS in Context: HPC, Life Sciences in the Cloud

Over the last few years, AWS has highlighted a number of large-scale genomics studies on their infrastructure, including the 1000 Genomes project and more focused genomics research efforts from companies like Novartis. To attract more, they have beefed up their regulatory appeal to make sharing personal health data (not to mention securing it) less of a concern for this privacy-aware market.

While these cases showcase the potential for genomics on AWS, researchers in the area have managed to get the data collection step in the DNA analysis pipeline down to a science. In other words, getting the data to the cloud is not necessarily a challenge. However, when it comes to efficiently processing the petabytes of sequence information to make meaningful connections in a way that demonstrates the often-touted economic and time to result benefits, there are still some shortcomings, at least according to researchers from Harvard Medical School, Stanford Medical School, and a number of other institutions.

For most large-scale genomics research, the problems can be parallelized nicely across as many compute engines as teams can throw at the application, but optimizing at extreme scale and developing a workflow are still challenges. To this end, the team of researchers tapped the Amazon cloud for a scalable framework to test the limits of genomics workflows. Supported by a grant from Amazon Web Services, they were able to show how a custom workflow they developed was able to reduce the cost of analysts of whole-genome data by 10x.

At its core, the project, called, COSMOS is a Python library designed to handle large-scale workflows that require a more formal description of pipelines and partitioning of jobs. Among the components are a UI for tracking the progress of jobs, abstraction of the job queuing system (to allow interface to multiple queuing systems) and fine-grained control over the workflow. While it has been benchmarked most extensively (and publicly) on AWS, it also runs on Google Compute Engine and on on-premises hardware.

COSMOS, tackles the problems that plague genomics workflows in two ways. As the researchers note, this happens via the implementation of "a highly parallelizable workflow that can be run quickly and efficiently on a large compute cluster—and can take advantage of AWS spot-instance pricing to reduce the cost per hour." Target medical breakthroughs include genetic insight into the exomes of epilepsy and myelomonocytic leukemia in addition to other broader genomic studies.

The performance tests were done using standard AWS EC2 nodes in conjunction with the MIT-developed StarCluster manager, which handles provisioning and closing down of nodes based on the job requirements. Also at the core of the approach is Grid Engine, which is managed through StarCluster and is present on each of the AWS nodes. The COSMOS framework also has a plugin that allows installation of the GlusterFS file system on each of the nodes.

The work has been going on since 2013, but is continuing to showcase the potential for clouds in genomics. COSMOS was developed specifically to support the clinical-time, next-generation sequencing (NGS) variant calling pipeline, but can be used to develop pipelines for any large-scale scientific workflow. It runs the parallelized workflow for optimum and scalable processing of NGS data (currently whole genome and whole exome) and supports projects such as the 6000 exome and genome analysis.

AWS got an early start in the life sciences by capturing early HPC cloud users who needed something different than their large scientific clusters could give. Their workloads did not always require the fast node-to-node communication other users but many workloads in life sciences were classified as HPC. AWS worked to publicly describe these use cases as it highlighted the computational capability and capacity, the ability to work with cloud-based software, and the addition of all the right security and regulatory pieces. While they have since branched the business out to nearly all other areas of HPC, life sciences is where AWS got an early foothold with HPC users—and it retains it to this day.

There is competition on the horizon for the life sciences and other scientific cloud users. Both Google and Microsoft have also extended new tools and services to these users, making 2016 a landmark year for HPC cloud competition.

Microsoft Azure Works to Capture HPC Cloud Share

While Amazon tends to get a great deal of airtime for its reach into the HPC market, teams at Microsoft have done extensive work over the last few years to make their cloud accessible, high performance, and packed with the right software for HPC users. Of greatest interest is the Microsoft HPC Pack, which is part of the Windows HPC Server suite. Although very few large-scale HPC centers use Windows Server exclusively, in the enterprise, there certainly are several use cases. Inside of this package are the deployment, administration, scheduling, and monitoring tools needed for both the Windows and Linux HPC cluster environments.

Microsoft has some noteworthy HPC use cases for Azure in number of areas, including financial risk modeling. The company recently helped Towers Watson move their computationally-intensive risk modeling to

THE STATE OF HPC CLOUD

the cloud. They have also worked with a number of engineering and design ISVs to allow design and simulation on the Azure cloud. On the life sciences front, Microsoft has worked with Wellcome Trust for genome analysis.

Microsoft has provided a breakdown of their HPC services via the list below.

Key features

- **High-performance hardware** – These instances are designed and optimized for compute-intensive and network-intensive applications, including high-performance computing (HPC) and batch applications, modeling, and large-scale simulations.

  For basic specs, storage capacities, and disk details, see Sizes for virtual machines. Details about the Intel Xeon E5-2667 v3 processor (used in the H-series) and Intel Xeon E5-2670 processor (in A8 - A11), including supported instruction set extensions, are at the Intel.com website.

- **Designed for HPC clusters** – Deploy multiple compute-intensive instances in Azure to create a stand-alone HPC cluster or to add capacity to an on-premises cluster. If you want to, deploy cluster management and job scheduling tools. Or, use the instances for compute-intensive work in another Azure service such as Azure Batch.

- **RDMA network connection for MPI applications** – A subset of the compute-intensive instances (H16r, H16mr, A8, and A9) feature a second network interface for remote direct memory access (RDMA) connectivity. This interface is in addition to the standard Azure network interface available to other VM sizes.

  This interface allows RDMA-capable instances to communicate with each other over an InfiniBand network, operating at FDR rates for H16r and H16mr virtual machines, and QDR rates for A8 and A9 virtual machines. The RDMA capabilities exposed in these virtual machines can boost the scalability and performance of certain Linux and Windows Message Passing Interface (MPI) applications. See Access to the RDMA network in this article for requirements.

Of course, like all companies in the cloud space, Microsoft wants to create a massive, general purpose offering that can serve all needs—HPC and machine learning just being subsets. Understanding how they do that with such a large competitor on the long-term horizon is of interest, especially matched with their investments in creating specialized hardware for key users.

A public cloud is, at its most basic level, a giant shared computing facility that spans a datacenter or multiple datacenters, and as such, it needs a kind of operating system of its own to make the collection of servers, storage, and switches behave as a single machine to both its users and to the company that is operating the cloud.

Given this, it is not at all surprising that after a few years working for its Azure public cloud team that Microsoft in September 2015 tapped Mark Russinovich, an operating system expert with deep and broad expertise, to be the chief technology officer in charge of the architecture of its cloud.

Azure has a number of different organizational levels within Microsoft, Russinovich works for the Azure Core Team, which is run by corporate vice president Jason Zander and which builds the infrastructure underpinning all of the services that run on Azure. (Other executives manage the services farther up the Azure stack.) This infrastructure spans millions of cores and exabytes of storage, and consumes many billions of dollars in investment each year to maintain and grow. Russinovich has a hand in designing the whole Azure infrastructure stack, from the custom systems and switches to the management and virtualization layers on top of them to the datacenters that house it all.

Russinovich has a long history of being a gadfly for Microsoft, and his appointment as Technical Fellow, the highest engineering title at the company, is yet another indication, along with Microsoft's adoption of Linux within its Azure infrastructure and as a first citizen alongside Windows Server on the Azure cloud, that the new Microsoft is keen on being more open as it seeks to transform its business from selling software licenses to providing cloud services. Russinovich took some time to chat with *The Next Platform* about the Azure platform he is helping to build for Microsoft, how it meshes with the vast installed base of Windows Server users worldwide, and how the company is embracing open source technologies such as Docker and Mesos to create a new abstraction layer for both private clouds and Azure.

To provide the most comprehensive description of where Azure is going across its cloud business, both for HPC and hyperscale, we have included an abbreviated (as relevant to HPC, machine learning, and large-scale enterprise) question and answer session with Russinovich, which was published in *The Next Platform (TNP)* in the summer of 2016.

TNP: How far ahead, if it all, is the software stack that you use to run the Azure cloud compared to the combination of Windows Server and Azure Pack that Microsoft sells to its enterprise customers to build their private clouds? Does Azure run ahead and test ideas and then they eventually get commercialized with Windows Server?

Russinovich: We co-design and we co-develop, and there are a couple of examples I can tell you about. The most public example is the work we are doing with Windows Server Containers, which is a joint effort between the Azure team and the Windows Server team. But when it comes to the virtualization platform itself, we will drive requirements and that means instead of building our own hypervisor, we leverage the Hyper-V hypervisor team that is part of the Windows Server core term as well as the virtual machine management team to get the functionality that Azure need. We work with them and validate that whatever they do meets cloud scale requirements, and then it goes right into Windows

Server and is made available to customers.

TNP: What is the main difference between running Windows at hyperscale as you do on Azure and running it at large scale as many large enterprises do? These are typically customers with thousands of nodes, not hundreds of thousands or more than a million nodes. Microsoft created Autopilot more than ten years ago to provision and manage the servers for its online servers, and a much-upgraded version of Autopilot runs Azure today, but this is not a commercial product and may not be appropriate as one, either. What are the big differences between what Azure does and what enterprises can do with Windows Server plus Azure Pack?

Russinovich: When it comes to Windows Server and Azure Pack versus Azure, a lot of the same technology is in both places. As much as we can, we give customers the same bits that we are running in Azure. I think the big difference is the automation at the scale that we operate at and how we do updates to the next platform, which is something that enterprises would do differently. Similarly with the way that we monitor the servers and keep track of repairs, and the way that we deploy updates to our fleet around the world are also different. With thousands of servers, you can use people to take care of repairing servers, but when you are doing it across millions of servers, you need to have automated processes to handle that.

When it comes to core technologies, just to give you one concrete example in software defined networking, the software load balancer that we have in Azure we are making available in Azure Pack and as part of Windows Server 2016.

TNP: Does Microsoft IT run on Azure at this point?

Russinovich: Microsoft IT has been on a migration to Azure over the past few years, and it has been an ongoing migration and at this point the company bet is on Azure. Any department or project that wants to run something on infrastructure other than Azure has to get an exception up at a very high level within the company. It is all roads lead to Azure, and we are migrating existing stuff.

TNP: For the past several years, it has been pretty obvious that Azure is not just about Windows, and that other technologies like the Linux operating system and Docker containers are key components of Azure. How important are these technologies and how much usage do they drive?

Russinovich: When we launched Azure infrastructure as a service in preview, we went out the door with Windows as well as Linux. We have seen tremendous growth in Linux usage on Azure. Starting as a Windows-only cloud, it had a perception to overcome and we had to convince people that we could support Linux as a first class citizen. Last fall, one out of every five virtual machines deployed on Azure was running Linux, and today it is one out of every four. And when it comes to our new virtual machine APIs, basically one out of every two or three is a Linux virtual machine.

And when it comes to Docker, we have been partnering very closely with Docker to bring Docker APIs and technologies to Windows Server, and that has been a year and a half collaboration. We work so closely with Docker that one of our engineers was the top contributor into the Docker GitHub repository from January through August of this year.

TNP: Can we talk a bit about the iron underneath Azure? You put out your second generation of Open Cloud Server machines at the Open Compute Summit in March, based on Intel "Haswell" Xeon E5 processors. What do you have cooking now? Are you looking at silicon photonics and future "Broadwell" and "Skylake" Xeons?

Russinovich: We are working on the next generation now and once that is ready, we will contribute that to the Open Compute Project. Silicon photonics and those other technologies are not ready yet, but we are obviously looking and working with those companies very closely and the second that they are viable there is no lag and we can bring that to Azure instantly. The servers that we have got in design now do not have silicon photonics in them. We just announced our DV2 Azure instances, which are on Haswell.

TNP: Windows client software runs on ARM processors, and if anyone knows how to flip a few bits to get a client operating system to load server applications, it is you. What are the prospects for ARM in the Azure cloud? Obviously, as is the case with all hyperscalers, you control your own code base and it is easier for you to deploy new architectures in the cloud than it is for enterprises do to inside their own datacenters.

Mark Russinovich: Just like we look at silicon photonics, we are looking at all technologies and seeing where they might be viable, and that is all I can say about it. We are definitely looking at ARM technologies and watching the evolution of them in the server space.

TNP: Do you think that most of the Windows Server installed base will have at least some services running on Azure?

Russinovich: I think we see that most of these customers already do. The interesting thing that I am seeing is that the transformation that is undergoing in the industry is at a pace that is faster than a lot of people imagine. When I started at Azure five years ago, nobody knew what IaaS, PaaS, or SaaS was. They knew about cloud, and they thought it was for other people and while they could see many of the benefits, they were only thinking they might move at some point in the future.

Today, it is "cloud first" at many companies, and ones that you would not expect it from, where there are mandates from the CEOs and CIOs to move to the public cloud as fast as possible. We are talking about initiatives over one or two years to migrate all of their applications. They want to cut costs, and this is especially true among financial firms, which are constrained by growth at this point. Of course, these companies are going to be in hybrid mode for a long time, because they have lots of applications to move or data they think is too sensitive to move. This is why we have such a big effort in Microsoft to support the hybrid mode.

We are seeing massive growth on all fronts: IaaS, PaaS, and SaaS. With infrastructure services, a lot of that is driven by lift and shift and by movements of applications where the customers want to support hybrid. But more and more, we see them taking advantage of platform services, because this is where the true value of the cloud comes. This instant, highly managed functionality would take a long while and a lot of money to manage if you were doing it yourself, such as database or event ingestion as a services. And we take it to even higher levels, with business verticals and machine learning applied to data analytics. And we of course have Dynamics and Office365, which is driving a huge amount of SaaS onto the Azure platform. SaaS is definitely an easy entry point. We see a lot of customers coming to the cloud first for Office365, and that makes them use Azure Active Directory, and then it is natural to use Azure for other cloud services from there.

In addition to talking about the new N series GPU-backed instances, Zander also rolled out new DV2 series instances based on Intel's "Haswell" Xeon E5 processors, which were announced last September. Specifically, the DV2 instances are based on the Xeon E5-2673 v3 processors, which appear to be a custom part with sixteen cores with a Turbo Boost speed bump to 3.2 GHz and a base clock speed of 2.4 GHz. In general, Zander said that the DV2 family of virtual machines would offer about

35 percent better performance than the D series VMs on Azure, Both the D and DV2 instances have relatively fast processors and flash-based SSDs for storage and are beefier than the entry A series, while the G series pack the most compute into an instance.

The base D1 v2 instance has a single core, 3.5 GB of memory, and 50 GB of flash for 15.5 cents per hour (about $115 per month), while the heaviest D14 v2 instance has sixteen cores, 112 GB of memory, and 800 GB of flash for $2.43 per hour (about $1,806 per month). These prices are a bit lower than what Microsoft was charging for the original D family Azure VMs, which have slower Xeon E5 processors and the same memory and storage capacities.

Starting October 1, 2016 Microsoft is reducing the prices on D series instances by 18 percent, to between 17.1 cents per hour for the D1 to $2.11 per hour for the D14 instance. That price cut makes the old D instances about 10 percent cheaper than the DV2 instances with skinnier memory and sometimes quite a bit deeper on instances with heavier memory. That means you have to do the math to figure out if you need to be on the D or DV2 instances, and it is not a simple yes or no. It depends – unless more is always better.

Google Ogles HPC, Large-Scale Enterprise Needs with Cloud

Search engine giant Google has invented so much sophisticated and scalable infrastructure for gathering, processing, and storing information that you cannot help it for wanting you to just consume what it has created as an abstracted platform service, just like the programmers at Google do.

But that is not how the world works, at least not yet. Even as the company's top brass talked at the Next

2016 conference in San Francisco about how its Cloud Platform was different from key competitors Amazon Web Services, Microsoft Azure, and IBM SoftLayer, and Rackspace Hosting, the discussion always drifted towards services and away from virtualized infrastructure where companies can do their own thing. This may get the hackles up for those who, like Google, think they can bring differentiation to their IT organizations at the infrastructure layer and all the way up the stack to applications. And Google is committed to offering infrastructure, platform, and software services across the board, and to its credit, it has set about exposing the services it uses internally so that others can buy them with metered pricing.

If you want to go through – or have to go through – the evolutionary stages that Google itself went through to create a massively scaled, largely automated set of infrastructure that makes it relatively easy to deploy applications, you can do it.

The biggest message coming out of Next 2016 is that Google is absolutely committed to the public cloud, and that it intends to be a contender against AWS and Azure, which have a similar scale in terms of the raw infrastructure they deploy but which have different levels of revenue derived cloud capacity and services. Last December, the company tapped Diane Greene, one of the co-founders of VMware, the server virtualization juggernaut that has built a tidy $6 billion business making X86 servers in the corporate datacenters of the world more efficient, to run the company's enterprise business, which includes Google Cloud Platform and a slew of applications, and interestingly, also puts her in charge of datacenters and their gear, with Urs Hölzle, senior vice president of technical infrastructure, reporting to Greene.

"We are serious about this business," said Greene during her keynote address, reminding everyone that

Google's parent company, now called Alphabet, invested $9.9 billion in capital equipment in 2015, with the vast majority of it being for its datacenters and the gear inside of it.

How much of this is dedicated to the Cloud Platform public cloud is not divulged, but it has to be a fairly small portion of it. Say it scales with revenues, then Alphabet's overall revenues of $74.5 billion last year would represent the bulk of that infrastructure spending, with Cloud Platform probably generating (we estimate) somewhere around $900 million in revenues in 2015 (but more than doubling annually unlike the overall Google.) Google's cloud infrastructure expenses are probably pretty small, maybe on the order of several hundred million dollars, perhaps as high as $1 billion, but are set to explode.

As part of a 2016 campaign to tell the world how serious Google is about the public cloud, the company announced that it had expanded its facilities in Oregon and added a new datacenter in Tokyo, and that by the end of 2017 it would add another ten facilities – a mix of its own datacenters and those hosted in co-location facilities. Google opened a datacenter region in South Carolina last year, and has three other facilities in Council Bluffs, Iowa, St. Ghislain, Belgium, and Changhua, Taiwan. Each region has three or four zones. This capacity is accessible through 77 different network integration points across the world, which also hook into the other Google datacenters that are not running Cloud Platform workloads and which hook users into the Google wide area network, which is called B4, that links its datacenters together.

But Google has come to realize, as have Amazon, Microsoft, and IBM, that regional laws and business practices often require for datacenters to be located closer to the businesses that use them, and companies are also sensitive to latencies and they want to have rented capacity closer to their users. Hence the investment in more datacenters in the coming two years.

Google did not say where it would be building these datacenters, but it stands to reason that there will be more geographic distribution than we have seen in the past. It is reasonable to expect for Google to add capacity at existing facilities that currently only run its own workloads as well as adding other co-lo capacity where appropriate or politically expedient. Google operates 14 datacenter regions of its own today. Microsoft operates 22 Azure regions and will be adding five more this year. AWS has 12 regions with a total of 33 availability zones and is adding five more regions with a total of eleven more zones this year. All zones are not created equal within cloud providers or across them, of course, but it is safe to assume that a facility has many tens of thousands of servers.

Having capacity distributed around the globe is going to be important if Cloud Platform is to reach the level of AWS, which has over 1 million customers and which hit $7.88 billion in revenues. But Google has some technology tricks up its sleeve that it thinks, in the long run, will make its cloud more appealing to enterprise customers and startups alike. It is also willing to compete on price, which Google absolutely can do based on the vastness of its infrastructure and the volumes at which it buys servers, storage, and switching.

Hölzle said in his presentation that the custom machine type virtual machines that Cloud Platform launched last year allowed the average customer to save about 19 percent on their compute bills versus having to buy specific instance types. Also, because Cloud Platform has per-minute pricing rather than hourly pricing for compute infrastructure, customers can see significantly more savings compared to other cloud providers.

"But cost is not the only thing," Hölzle added. "When you are thinking about picking a cloud provider for the next decade, innovation and the quality of the underlying infrastructure is just as important. In fact, if you are picking that cloud provider for a decade, innovation might be the most important part. So it is time to look at what is next. Over the next five years, I think that we will see more change in computing and in cloud than we have seen in the last decade or two – literally an explosion in innovation."

Hölzle said he is basing that idea on a well-known effect in biological systems, where once a basic system is in place it enables evolution to accelerate. (He did not name this phenomenon nor did he mention anything about punctuated equilibrium or mass extinction.) "We are entering a similarly explosive period in cloud computing innovation right now, and as more software gets woven into our daily lives and into your companies, you all face the same challenges that Google has faced for many years – mainly to create more functional, easy to use applications, operate them at scale, and operate them at scale cheaply, efficiently, and securely."

The answer is to automate everything, which Google has largely done, and that is why it is banging the "No Ops" mantra today as the hype around DevOps – making developers responsible for not just creating, but deploying and maintaining applications in production – continues to grow. Hölzle said that developers spend way too much time administering their setups, and he predicted it would be easy to run "even ambitious applications" at scale. (Google knows a thing or two about this, as does Microsoft and Amazon, of course.) With App Engine, DataFlow, Kubernetes, and other services on the Google cloud, he said Google was well on the way to accomplishing this goal for its cloud customers as it has long since done internally for its own software developers.

What Google is really after – and what it is selling to customers as their future because this is the experience inside of Google already – is something Hölzle is calling the "serverless architecture," which means making the infrastructure absolutely invisible. In the past two decades, we have moved from physical machines in a co-location facility to virtual machines in a cloud datacenter, from a purchase order to an API call, which he said was a very profound change but that the basic building blocks of the virtual datacenters had not changed yet.

"It is still extraordinarily complex to orchestrate these building blocks together at scale. Developers have to think about things other than making their applications great – do we have enough servers, are they all patched, did we prepurchase too much capacity. In the virtualized datacenter world, this never gets easier. And actually it is a bit crazy that today's cloud is based on all of the physical limitations that were created twenty years ago. It is like the virtual datacenter today still has a manual choke."

Google was there ten years ago, but then it created software containers for Linux and the Borg container scheduler and a slew of other technologies that are the underpinnings of its infrastructure stack today, which insulates developers from worrying about frameworks and capacity planning and to focus on storing data and chewing on it for insight.

Which brings Google, and perhaps its cloud customers, full circle to the platform cloud that it always wanted to sell to enterprises in the first place. That was a hard sell in 2008, but it might be a whole lot easier in 2016, we think. And if you want raw virtual machines and containers, well, Google can expose those to you as well if you want to do it the hard way.

But back to HPC… In times long since passed, when cloud was the latest, greatest hype machine, a steady wave of "cloud enablement" companies came to fore, promising secure ease as users tiptoed across the firewall. As we have seen over the last several years, a great many of these have been absorbed by infrastructure providers or have dissolved into mist.

The startups that managed to make it past the initial cloud boom and managed to carve out a niche, most successfully as highly-touted partners of Amazon, Microsoft, and Google cloud platforms have had to work hard to stand out. For some, it helped to specialize, as was the case with Cycle Computing, which found its early footing by tapping into the supercomputing set. For this specific group of users in the high performance computing market, the initial worries about cloud security could oftentimes take a backseat to suspicious about what the virtualization overhead meant for performance. And that, coupled with large simulation datasets, made the HPC cloud market a tough one to play in.

But play they did, moving from some early use cases with cloud-based HPC applications into the demanding workloads from the life sciences industry. From large pharma companies to smaller research firms and their sequencing needs, Cycle Computing was able to establish a reputation as a critical middle layer in the HPC to cloud transition. The company counts most of the major companies doing large-scale drug discovery as customers, which means that many of these have already found a comfortable fit in the Amazon cloud.

Since the mid-2000s, when they first came onto the scene, Cycle's business of "enablement" has meant patching together some sophisticated middleware to onboard tough applications for large core-count jobs. For instance, more recently, the company spun up a 70,000 core cluster for hard drive maker, HGST to model their new helium drives in high resolution and last year they put their brains (and software) behind a petaflop-capable cloud-based machine for Schrodinger for a molecular dynamics application. The key to both of these stories, as well as their other use cases, is that they are helping companies like Amazon prove out that tricky cloud math or rather, when it makes sense to do something in-house versus push it out to cloud infrastructure. The costs that underlie this, namely the management, procurement, and various optimizations are shouldered by Cycle, which has been fine-tuning its approach on a user-by-user basis on the Amazon cloud.

As of today, Cycle's opportunity to move outside of Amazon's borders and capture a potential base of new users expanded. The company's CEO, Jason Stowe, shared news of the new hooks for the Google cloud with *The Next Platform*, noting that there are many new use cases they expect will open in the coming months. While they have continued to find new large users through their Amazon partner status, including most recently, the Food and Drug Administration (FDA), expanding beyond that base makes sense and could them secure more long-term users. Stowe estimates that for every long-term user of their CycleCloud service there are 2X-3X that use the cloud (and their middleware) for a single major undertaking where in-house resources aren't enough.

These ties with Google Compute Engine are being announced in tandem with two related news items, one from Cycle, the other from Google. First is the fact that Cycle Computing has been working with the Broad Institute to make the move to the Google cloud for a cancer research workload that ate 50,000 cores on GCE. The second item is that Google announced that its preemptible VMs, which were launched in beta several months ago (and are akin to spot instance pricing on AWS) are entering full availability. Interestingly, Stowe explained that it was this very feature inside GCE that pushed the Broad Institute the Google Cloud way, although work between Google and the Broad Institute has been ongoing in previous months for other workloads.

The Broad Institute ran what amounted to thirty years of cancer research calculations in just a few hours based on a decade's worth of sequenced or genotyped biological samples—1.4 million to be exact. With Cycle's help, they were able to scale to this level in just a few weeks, taking advantage of preemptible VMs for price reductions, even if it means there is always a chance their workload could be interrupted (we have a longer piece coming this morning featuring a chat with Paul Nash, Google's product manager for GCE describing this). As Chris Dwan, acting director of IT at the Broad Institute described, "this kind of cloud-based infrastructure helps us remove some of the local computing barriers that can stand in the way. Flexible processing power allows us to think on a much larger scale."

While use cases like the Broad Institute's genomics workloads are in Cycle's sweet spot (and are a target market for cloud providers), Stowe says that Cycle is seeing momentum in more areas, including manufacturing. Although the company's start was in research and life sciences, there is far less concern about the "older" topics like security and more of a sense that the real challenge is making sure it is possible to efficiently balance workloads between what stays in-house and what is sent to the cloud. Cycle's service helps manage this via policies and with more hooks into other workload management frameworks, including Univa's Grid Engine, which was used in the Broad Institute example, they plan to keep broadening their reach through wider integration and orchestration with schedulers and cloud provider use cases.

On that orchestration front, the goal for the Broad was to ensure they were getting the necessary scale and performance, but of great importance was the pricing benefits they hoped to capture from the preemptible VMs. This is a similar challenge for Cycle in terms what the company faced in rolling out support for spot pricing inside of AWS, but the fundamental concept is the same.

We have a representation for these clustered applications, it is not unlike a container approach in concept," Stowe explains. "Our software takes sets of hosts and sets of roles and makes it so you can consistently orchestrate them in different infrastructures. From a practical standpoint, things like a Grid Engine cluster or a parallel shared file system or a Spark cluster or any other number of examples, all of those are just clustered applications with a head node and read/write nodes and maybe a shared file system–all those roles we abstract in a generic way, and we can orchestrate all of that at scale."

IBM's Stake in Public Cloud

To discuss IBM's future in the cloud market, for both enterprise and high performance computing applications, it is necessary to look at the overall business on the system, software, and cloud sides. Unlike Amazon (and more like Microsoft) IBM has a significant software and services division that provides a useful entry path for long-time customers.

More than anything else, over its long history in the computing business, IBM has been a platform company and say what you will about the woes it has had through several phases of its history, what seems obvious is that when Big Blue forgets this it runs into trouble.

If you stare at its quarterly financial results long enough, you can still see that platform company looking back at you, even through the artificially dissected product groups the company has used for the past decade and the new ones that IBM is using starting in 2016.

It is important to remember that even after all the divestures of its System x server business to Lenovo and its Microelectronics chip business to Globalfoundries last year, IBM's systems business is still a much larger platform company than Amazon Web Services and is many times larger than Google Compute Platform and Microsoft Azure (at least the part that is selling raw capacity and services to end users). In 2014, when IBM still sold servers based on Intel Xeon processors, that systems business generated around $33.3 billion, including servers, storage, operating systems, transaction processing software, integration middleware, technical support, and financing of this gear, and in 2015, after divesting itself of that Xeon server business and the associated revenue streams, the overall systems business fell by 14.5 percent to $28.5 billion.

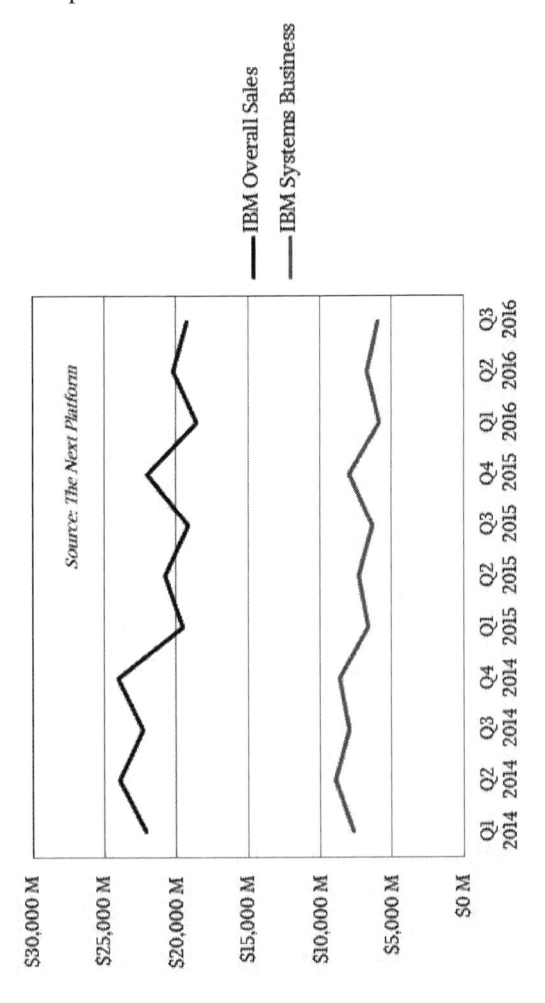

This is still 3.6X as large as AWS, although the two are arguably very different animals indeed, and AWS is growing at 80 percent a year and if IBM's systems business continues to shrink, they will be roughly the same size at $25 billion a year in 2018.

That will be a remarkable day, should it come to pass.

Not at all ironically, IBM is trying to become more like AWS, with its acquisition of SoftLayer being just part of that, as well as a supplier of on-demand, cloud-based software for marketing, advertising, and analytics. But these nascent businesses are utterly dwarfed by the tradition System z and Power Systems platforms that the company still sells and the DB2 database and WebSphere middleware that dominates on these systems and is often sold on machines made by others to do transaction processing.

The important thing for Big Blue is that these legacy platform businesses continue to generate revenues and profits as the rest of the company undergoes another wrenching transformation. It would be easy to pick on IBM, but its peers among the largest IT suppliers (including Sun Microsystems, Hewlett Packard Enterprise, Dell, and Microsoft) have arguably had no more easy a time of it in the past two decades.

What is concerning is that during the first quarter ended in March, the mainframe and Power Systems cycles seemed to run out of steam and it looks like there will be quite a wait until the next round of System z14 and Power9 machines are out the door – we don't know when the next mainframe cycle begins, but IBM did not launch Power8+ systems this year as its roadmaps had suggested it would and is just adding NVLink interconnects for GPU accelerators to the existing Power8 chips that have been around since 2014. It is not clear that IBM's customers need a new chip right now, or its partners in the OpenPower collective, for that matter, but what is important is that an updated Power chip implies a boost in price/performance, which would have gone a long way toward helping Power-based machines compete better against the new "Broadwell" Xeon E5 v4 processors that Intel just launched. In any event, a 24-core Power9 chip aimed at two-socket systems is coming next year, timed roughly to coincide with Intel's "Skylake" Xeon E5 v5 processors, so this is where the real battle will take place. This should also be when companies like Google and Rackspace Hosting deploy Power-based systems in their infrastructure in reasonable volumes, and perhaps we will see some big design wins for ARM-based servers, too.

We think 2017 and 2018 are going to be a very interesting year for systems, and we think that IBM is gearing up the Power platform with its partners to get a bigger slice of the pie while at the same time doing everything it can to shore up its mainframe business to help fuel the transformation of its platform business.

In 2016, IBM's overall revenues continued to trend down as did its core systems business, which depending on the quarter accounts for about a third of its overall revenues. IBM still sells a lot of services, from systems integration to application hosting, that we are not counting in this core systems business, and we are also not adding in its SoftLayer cloud because we don't actually know how large it is but it is probably around an order of magnitude lower than the sale of systems to large enterprises, governments, and service providers that constitutes most of the IBM systems business.

Starting in 2016, IBM is carving its business into five main groups. Its Global Business Services and Global Financing units are essentially unchanged from their prior characterization in financial reports.

	Q1 2014	Q2 2014	Q3 2014	Q4 2014	Q1 2015	Q2 2015	Q3 2015	Q4 2015	Q1 2016	Q2 2016	Q3 2016
Systems Hardware Revenue	$2,142 M	$3,014 M	$2,432 M	$2,404 M	$1,657 M	$2,056 M	$1,491 M	$2,370 M	$1,243 M	$1,617 M	$1,192 M
Systems Hardware Gross Profit	$729 M	$1,197 M	$827 M	$1,193 M	$739 M	$992 M	$668 M	$1,137 M	$577 M	$745 M	$440 M
Hardware Gross Profit Margin	34.0%	39.7%	34.0%	49.6%	44.6%	48.2%	44.8%	48.0%	46.4%	46.1%	36.9%
Operating Systems Revenue	$567 M	$579 M	$565 M	$592 M	$484 M	$485 M	$482 M	$522 M	$432 M	$539 M	$434 M
Operating Systems Gross Profit	$496 M	$511 M	$494 M	$539 M	$435 M	$442 M	$435 M	$478 M	$381 M	$488 M	$385 M
OS Gross Profit Margin	87.5%	88.3%	87.4%	91.0%	89.9%	91.1%	90.2%	91.6%	88.3%	90.5%	88.8%
Total Systems Revenue	$2,709 M	$3,593 M	$2,997 M	$2,996 M	$2,141 M	$2,541 M	$1,973 M	$2,892 M	$1,675 M	$2,156 M	$1,626 M
Total Systems Pre-Tax Income	-$201 M	$560 M	$247 M	$777 M	$261 M	$538 M	$248 M	$674 M	-$10 M	$229 M	$136 M
Systems Pre-Tax Income Percent	-6.8%	14.4%	7.5%	24.6%	11.3%	19.7%	11.4%	21.7%	-0.5%	10.6%	7.8%

The Systems group that IBM has created, which we detail in the table above, brings together the server and storage hardware it sells with the operating systems that were put into the former Software Group, which has been disbanded. IBM sold $1.68 billion in servers in the first quarter to customers, and another $212 million to other units that use its hardware as the basis for appliances. (The first quarter is perhaps a better proxy for IBM than the other two, with mainframe sales at the tail end of their cycle.) Within the external customers, $1.24 billion of that was for servers and storage, down 25 percent, and $432 million was for operating systems, down 10.7 percent.

IBM's operating system sales are dominated by its System z mainframes, which are paid for on a monthly basis and are therefore very stable and almost like an annuity. Sales of its own AIX and IBM i operating systems are perpetual licenses with monthly maintenance fees, and the company also resells Red Hat, SUSE Linux, and Canonical Linux distributions on its System z and Power Systems iron. IBM said that its System z revenues were off 43 percent in the quarter, which is a bigger drop than the tail end of a mainframe cycle typically gets, and added that after four quarters of growth in 2015, the Power Systems business posted a 14 percent decline in Q1 2016. IBM's tape, disk, and flash storage business had a 7 percent drop, and IBM did not elaborate further.

This System group posted a gross profit of $958 million in the first quarter, with the operating system portion being very profitable, with 88.3 percent gross margins. Hardware has lower gross margins, at 46.4 percent, but this is to be expected. The overall Systems group did have a pre-tax loss of $10 million once corporate overhead costs were allocated to it, which is not good news.

The other new group is called Cognitive Solutions, and this includes a slew of transaction processing software, including databases and transaction monitors, that had been previously part of Software Group as well as data analytics tools such as the Cognos and SPSS statistical modeling tools and the BigInsights Hadoop distribution. In the first quarter, this part of IBM drove just under $4 billion in sales externally and another $668 million to other groups at the company. IBM sold $1.28 billion in transaction processing software externally in the quarter, and $2.7 billion in cognitive software, which includes databases and analytics tools as well as its nascent Watson analytics platform. While this business posted a pre-tax income of over $1 billion, it is down by 33.7 percent compared to the year ago period.

The final part of the "new" IBM is called Technical Services and Cloud Platform group, which has all kinds of infrastructure and technical support services and, for some reason, its WebSphere and other integration software is also put into this category. This is now the largest part of IBM, with $8.4 billion in sales in the first quarter and fell by 1.5 percent. Because of restructuring, this group had a big drop in pre-tax income, off 77.2 percent to $258 million in the quarter.

The SoftLayer public cloud, which is not broken out separately, is part of this final group, and all IBM said about it was that SoftLayer had "double digit" revenue growth in the period. Within the Technology Services and Cloud Platform group, IBM said that it had $1.2 billion in cloud-related revenues, up 50 percent year-on-year, and that the run rate on its "as a Service" products running on its own infrastructure hit $3.7 billion from within the TS&CP group.

Across all of its groups, cloud products drove $2.6 billion in sales (up 36 percent) and those cloud services (infrastructure, platform, and software as a service) had an annualized run rate of $5.4 billion, up 46 percent. IBM is focusing on the growth here, obviously, and we think it is probably being very generous with the definition of "cloud" when it comes to mainframe and Power Systems sales, too. Again across all of its groups, analytics products and services drove $4.2 billion in sales, up 9 percent. These two areas are the main drives for the company's "strategic imperatives," which also includes mobile and social application development tools and security software.

As we have pointed out before, IBM's "real" systems business is considerably larger than its systems hardware and operating system sales suggest. To get a sense of the size of that "real" business, we added up systems hardware, operating systems, transaction processing and database software, plus 90 percent of its integration software sales and 75 percent of its tech support and financing revenues. Add it all up, and as we pointed out already, and this is about a third of the company's overall revenues in any given quarter.

And here is the chart that gives you a better sense of how the revenues for each component of IBM's "real" systems business are trending:

THE STATE OF HPC CLOUD

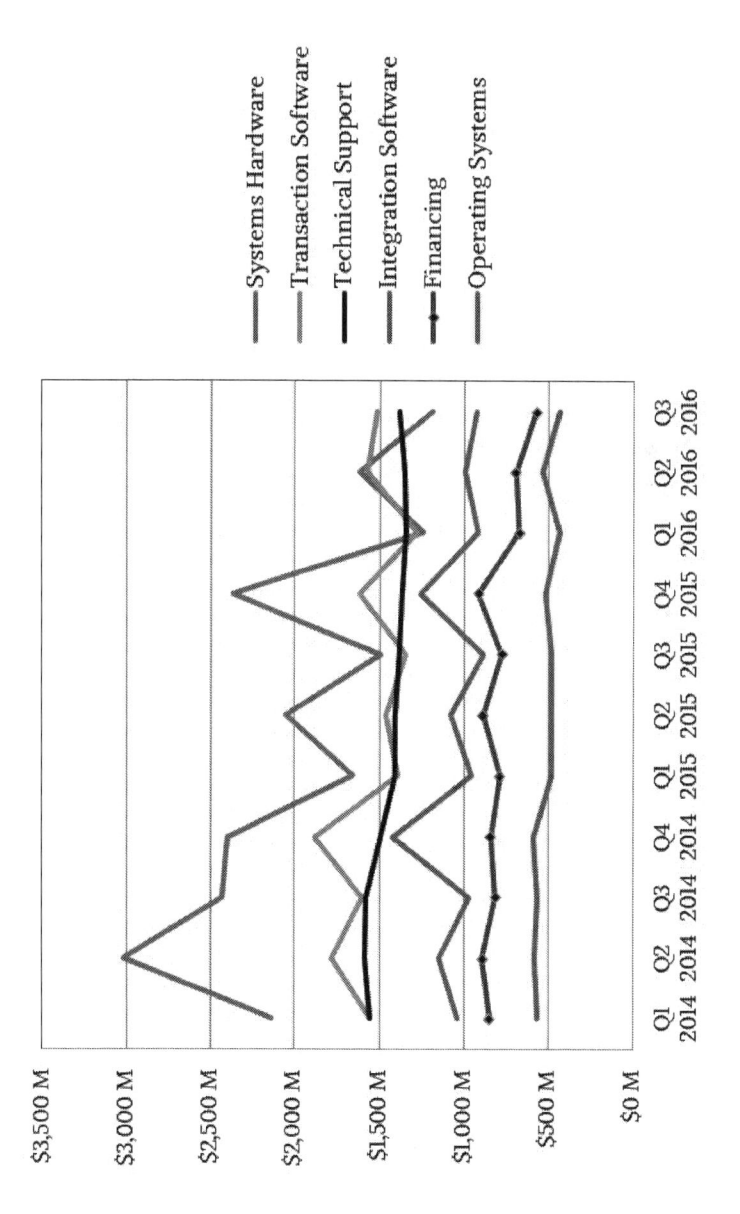

The numbers are all down over the past two years and change. This is not a good thing, obviously.

What we want to know is what the future IBM platform will look like and how it will grow. IBM's future is not the mainframe business, even though it is lucrative. We think that IBM needs to put a stake in the ground and build a substantial Power-based variant of SoftLayer that makes its case for that platform. It cannot wait until Google and Rackspace Hosting come around and adopt Power9-based machines in 2017 or 2018, although that will certainly help. Perhaps this is the plan, and perhaps this is how it will sell a lot of its Power Systems capacity in the future.

IBM's cloud revenues, which are spread across its various operating groups, include revenues from its SoftLayer public cloud as well as virtualized and orchestrated systems that it sets up on premises for customers plus various software that IBM makes available on its public cloud or those on premises private clouds. For example, IBM's Bluemix implementation of the Cloud Foundry platform cloud has only been available on SoftLayer, but IBM has just made it available for private clouds.

SoftLayer is now operating 28 of its own datacenters, and if you do the math, those facilities have the capacity to host 335,500 servers. That does not mean, however, that SoftLayer has that many machines. As of the summer of 2014, SoftLayer had around 120,000 machines and had plans to roughly double that number as it spent $1.2 billion to build out the SoftLayer cloud globally. The company has traditionally added around 20,000 machines a year, but that was back when it had only 13 datacenters a year and a half ago. SoftLayer could have anywhere between 175,000 and 200,000 servers by now, we estimate.

While IBM is investing heavily in its platforms, it still has a sizable and profitable systems business, and its mainframe and Power Systems are platforms in their own right and the foundation of some of the higher-level platforms that Schroeter is referring to. (IBM's Watson and Watson Health analytics runs on Power-based systems inside its SoftLayer cloud, for instance.) You have to peel apart IBM's revenues in each of its groups and divisions to get a sense of that systems business – something IBM itself should do if it wanted to show what a large systems business it still has even after selling off its X86 server business in 2014.

In many areas, IBM's cloud, both hardware and software, is tuned for Watson. Amazon, Google, and Microsoft are all seeing how their early investments in HPC hardware are paying off as well. Accordingly, we will end our analysis of where the large public cloud players stand in the market here by noting that all of the companies we just mentioned are seeing HPC as part of a much larger whole, especially as more analytics users turn an eye to machine learning. For now, it is not enough to simply have racks of CPUs, but instead of to provide a heterogeneous offering where users can quickly onboard.

Although the major public cloud providers have put effort into capturing HPC end users by providing software, tools, and hardware, the impetus has been about more than just sating the performance needs of HPC. Providing users with access to GPUs means the potential for a larger deep learning and machine learning base. In fact, because of the momentum in that area, GPUs are seeing a major uptick. We suspect there might be similar uptake with FPGAs over the next few years, assuming the programming tools are provided to make them easier to use. In short, machine learning has given HPC efforts a shot in the arm as far as the major cloud providers are concerned.

Of course, this takes far more than simply providing the infrastructure to make machine learning and HPC happen at scale. No summary of the year in HPC cloud is sufficient without a look at some of the defining tools and trends. Containers are a large story this year, but so too are tales of onboarding complex applications using a defined toolchain and approach. This brings to us to an important sub-section in the context of public and private clouds.

Making HPC Clouds Work: Onboarding and Tools

Many startups have come and gone since the early days of cloud, but when it comes to those that started small and grown organically with the expansion of use cases, Cycle Computing still stands tall.

Tall being relative, of course. As with that initial slew of cloud startups, a lot of investment money has sloshed around as well. As Cycle Computing CEO, Jason Stowe, reminds *The Next Platform*, the small team started with an $8,000 credit card bill with sights on the burgeoning needs of scientific computing users in need of spare compute capacity and didn't take funding until this year. The company took the $25 million in revenue it has gathered since 2008 and pushed it back into the business. Cycle now has broadly expanded its reach with enterprise customers while continuing with large-scale scientific and technical computing customers.

Stowe says Cycle has had three record quarters in a row and while it cannot report what revenue figure its 3X year-over-year growth represents, he says it is better than he could have dreamed when Cycle was digging in with the first tentative users of cloud—back in the days when managing hybrid resources was still a big challenge. Stowe says that while indeed, the cloud providers are making it easier to onboard and run applications, having an edge with an engineering team that understands the ins, outs, and pitfalls—and translates those into smart middleware that can seamlessly scale across the "infinite" resources of cloud is still necessary, especially for enterprise customers.

"The story hasn't changed much in some ways since those early days. People are still looking to take advantage of any infrastructure available—both internal and external. They don't want to wait for compute; they want to ask questions at any scale and get results back immediately. And for end users, there needs to be a toolchain that allows a seamless hybrid environment as well as all the benchmarking and other tools to make sure they're only getting the best of what is available."

Cycle already has a number of use cases in research, life sciences, and manufacturing, but one growth area is insurance and enterprise analytics. Most recently, the company worked with NASA's Center for Climate Simulation and the University of Minnesota on a carbon emissions study using their own in-house middleware to talk to AWS resources. This unique workload used up to 5,000 cores with 43 TB of data pushed through cost less than $2,000. Key to this low cost (relative to the amount of work) was the use of spot instances on the Amazon cloud.

In this case, spot instances worked out well—as it has for other customers Cycle works with. "Spot is usable for whole classes of workloads. In this case, many were 12-hour jobs. A lot of people say that's too long to consider using spot with AWS (or pre-emptible instances from Google) but we found we could run the whole workload without worry. In these 12-hour jobs, maybe 25 percent of the VMs were interrupted and had to be re-run. But the cost savings far outstripped this," Stowe explains. "The message is that just because a job takes longer than an hour doesn't mean you don't want to use spot instances."

This insight is what makes Cycle interesting to talk to. They are working with diverse, sometimes complex applications that span both the compute-intensive and data-intensive realms. This means they have developed a keen sense, especially with their own internal benchmarking efforts, about which clouds and configurations tend to perform best for broad classes of applications. While Stowe said they all have benefits, there is still no hard and fast rule about which instance type or cloud provider is best. Everything depends on the workload—and that means it's necessary to run benchmarks and take a close look at applications before getting started. Many of Cycle's customers come to them with a sense of which provider to use, but Cycle's teams help refine those decisions based on cost, time to result, and other factors.

Overall, Stowe says that when it comes to the various cloud providers they work with, there are some standout features. Azure's InfiniBand options are attractive for some customers, but he says the networks on Google and AWS are also good. "Azure is good for more traditional simulations; those workloads run well in that environment." And on the AWS side, there are features the team has rolled out to make cloud more cost-effective, most notably Spot. Still, he says for Google's part, they are working hard to be just as competitive on both the hardware and price points with a recent 33 percent price cut for their pre-emptible instances. "With Google, those areas, matched with their monthly usage discounting means they have a good cost impact as well as the performance."

Even still, it is difficult to make sweeping generalizations. "There are some folks who say that one application should always get a particular instance type but this is not true in our experience. Different users of different applications require different RAM ratios, requirements for performance characteristics, and other factors. You can draw broad strokes by knowing what your application needs, but mileage may vary and it is critical to test before production," Stowe says.

Stowe says that even as they have watched cloud use cases expand and the story remain mostly unchanged, there's another element that's not changing. "People are still thinking about their applications in terms of mirroring their internal and external environments. But shared infrastructure—the cloud—means that's no longer necessary."

Even though he says this is a widely known thing about the possibilities cloud opens up, there is still some catching up to do in the user community. "When you move to the cloud, you don't have to repeat that shared infrastructure metaphor anymore. Budget spend widths and alerts can be set with managed controls so everyone has their own playground and powers it down at the end of the day." This is still new to some enterprises, and while the operational benefits are clear, new customers are looking to this model for their development and other teams. "This is where the puck is going. Every member of a team having their own supercomputer. There is still an opportunity here."

Cycle Computing was quick to spot the initial opportunity of cloud and has been out in front of several of the largest public cloud uses to date, particularly with AWS. Even though the various cloud providers continue to build (and acquire) tools to create a similar streamlined onramp for large applications, Cycle has persisted—growing its cloud partners, bottom line, big name use cases, and of course, its legacy as one of the few companies that made it past the first heavy wave of cloud startup cuts.

It stands to reason that over the coming years, services like Cycle's that rooted an early foothold in helping users with complex HPC workflows tap into the benefits of cloud in both a full-on and hybrid capacity, will continue to flourish. This will likely be the case as well with companies that are eager to deploy machine learning or deep learning efforts using GPUs, which might not be familiar in the cloud or otherwise. In short, there is still no end in sight for those who provide services to help users push their applications to the cloud, especially for HPC cloud users.

On that note, another newer trend has offered a gateway to cloud adoption on the part of HPC end users. Containers, while not new, have seen a remarkable uptick in interest and adoption. While this can be a tricky approach for HPC centers that have multiple workflows, what it means for application sharing, portability, utilization, and collaboration is not to be discounted.

Over the last couple of years, Docker has become an increasingly popular tool for web-scale companies like eBay, but it appears to finally be catching on for some supercomputing centers. While there is additional complexity built into most HPC stacks, the desire to use Docker matched with key HPC-specific middleware makers' know-how about the specific needs is creating a new wave of tools—and demand.

Even though containers are finally receiving mainstream IT attention following the success of Docker, they are not a new concept, and are definitely not a fresh concept in high performance computing. From workload resource isolation, process tracking, job controlling, and checkpoint and restart functions, they have been a go-to, but now several HPC middleware companies are embracing it as part of their approach to HPC datacenter management.

During the 2016 OpenPower Summit, held in conjunction with the GPU Technology Conference, IBM outlined its approach to moving Docker into the Platform LSF workload management tooling, we got a closer look into how HPC-specific tuning for Docker has been built into one of the more popular schedulers in the segment from Sam Sanjabi, Advisory Software Engineer for IBM Platform Computing.

The way LSF works with Docker is similar to how other companies with HPC workload management tools and schedulers are integrating it. In essence, as seen below, the administrator creates Docker images which might have two versions of the same application and pop those into the registry. When the user submits a job to the scheduler, they might submit both versions and let the scheduler pull the appropriate image into the execution node to run inside the Docker container. The value here, as it's been proven out in mainstream IT and now HPC is that the admin's job becomes far simpler than before in that she is freed from deploying the many applications that might be running on the cluster—it becomes a matter of creating the Docker images, moving them into the repository, then allowing the scheduler, in this case LSF, orchestrate the rest.

The case for having a more sophisticated approach to managing resources and applications is especially important in HPC where there might be thousands of nodes with different hardware, memory, OS, and other characteristics that are tuned for different workloads. LSF and other HPC schedulers are already primed for pulling the right resources for the job based on extensive policies but as a monolithic scheduler, this is still not a breeze on the application front.

The benefits of Docker as implemented within the Platform LSF scheduler are the same that the general IT community is espousing, but again, it's a matter of scale and complexity. Again, HPC centers are often working with a wide range of demanding applications and hardware configurations, so having something to keep that in check is useful. At the core, however, Docker as built into a workload manager like LSF means resource guarantees and performance isolation (using the same concept of Linux control groups), with the addition of providing application encapsulation and the ability to seamlessly jump from different systems (including other clusters or bursting into a cloud resource) without having to bother with changing all the libraries across those other systems. If Docker is installed, users pull the images to the new host and run.

The real benefit of this approach for HPC centers, however is that different versions of applications can co-exist in the same environment without making the admin remember the different paths for all the different versions for a particular host. This also means it's repeatable, all of which is leading to the argument that this is a much more lightweight, high performance, and transparent way of handling multiple workload and environment complexity than one could get with doing the same thing with virtual machines.

On that note, there was a rather compelling study from IBM Research that took a close look at how different container and virtual machine approaches rank for HPC workloads. There are several such comparison available, in part because since Linux can support both virtual machines and containers, but this was one of the few without vendor influence. Using a host of different workloads that stressed memory, CPU, and I/O in different ways, the team found that when using KVM as the main hypervisor and Docker to handle containers, containers showed equal or better performance than virtual machines in almost every instance.

Workload		Native	Docker	KVM-untuned	KVM-tuned
PXZ (MB/s)		76.2 [±0.93]	73.5 (-4%) [±0.64]	59.2 (-22%) [±1.88]	62.2 (-18%) [±1.33]
Linpack (GFLOPS)		290.8 [±1.13]	290.9 (-0%) [±0.98]	241.3 (-17%) [±1.18]	284.2 (-2%) [±1.45]
RandomAccess (GUPS)		0.0126 [±0.00029]	0.0124 (-2%) [±0.00044]	0.0125 (-1%) [±0.00032]	Tuned run not warranted
Stream (GB/s)	Add	45.8 [±0.21]	45.6 (-0%) [±0.55]	45.0 (-2%) [±0.19]	
	Copy	41.3 [±0.06]	41.2 (-0%) [±0.08]	40.1 (-3%) [±0.21]	
	Scale	41.2 [±0.08]	41.2 (-0%) [±0.06]	40.0 (-3%) [±0.15]	
	Triad	45.6 [±0.12]	45.6 (-0%) [±0.49]	45.0 (-1%) [±0.20]	

The authors of the study note that even with these results, both the virtual machines and the Docker containers did require some sizable tuning for I/O-heavy operations, which can be seen above. "Although containers themselves have almost no overhead, Docker is not without performance gotchas," the IBM researchers caution. "Docker volumes have noticeably better performance than files stored in AUFS. Docker's NAT also introduces overhead for workloads with high packet rates—these features represent a tradeoff between ease of management and performance and should be considered on a case by case basis."

Accordingly, there are several HPC workload management and scheduler tools that are equipped with Docker aside from IBM Platform LSF. Adaptive Computing is another vendor that offers hooks into Docker containers and in recent conversations Univa, which is the commercial entity providing support for Grid Engine, told us that it is hard at work on its own Docker implementation.

There has been quite a lot of Docker momentum in the datacenter over the last year, and a strong companion effort to move containers into a wider range of user bases. But for high performance computing, the container approach for supercomputing sites has been weaker—and for several good reasons.

Despite some of the efforts from workload and resource management companies like IBM Platform Computing and Univa, there is still an uphill road ahead, but an effort based at the National Energy Research Scientific Computing Center (NERSC) is set to change that, and open a Docker-like approach for a larger set of HPC users. The approach, called Shifter, takes all the best elements of Docker and wraps them in a more HPC friendly package and will be open sourced to push into more HPC centers.

The question at hand, however, is what is so wrong with Docker that NERSC decided to move past it and build something new, but it is more of an extension off a workable tool, according to Shifter co-creator, Doug Jacobson. In essence, Shifter generates read-only images for users to deploy on HPC platforms, but Docker is not cut out of the picture entirely as it is the way these images are generated. As Jacobsen says, there is little reason to reinvent the wheel here since Docker already has a well-designed and documented way of letting people easily create and maintain existing images that can then be pushed into the cloud via Docker Hub or a private onsite hub. It is also good, he says, at solving a lot of interesting problems in the area of managing large parallel file systems—something HPC centers like NERSC certainly have.

Jacobsen, who is now a computer engineer at NERSC, used to be one of the center's bioinformatics and recalls installing four hundred different software packages for bioinformatics workloads. These were complex stacks with difficult dependency traits and ultimately, users did not care about the options of using different versions of software—they just wanted their code to run. When the team first started working with Docker containers, the idea that these users could bring their own defined image and install in a simple environment—a move that was revolutionary in terms of productivity, Jacobsen says. "We see no reason why people should need to have these complex paths to use our systems. They just cause performance, understanding, and other problems. Here, you bring your own software and container and while there are some modifications that have to happen still, new users can get going much faster."

But why re-invent the wheel at all if Docker is a strong tool for users in HPC center? Jacobsen tells *The Next Platform* they have used it with a number of smaller of HPC clusters. However, it turns out that there are two fatal flaws for Docker on a big high performance computing system like the Cray Edison supercomputer, for example. And these problems boil down to security and for the larger scope of HPC users at other sites, "simple" Linux versioning as well as a few other issues crop up with weighty parallel file systems.

"Docker has met the needs of a lot of user communities, but for a lot of HPC sites, the fact that it requires Linux kernel version 3.10 (and the previous required 3.08) this leaves a lot of centers behind. There are plenty of HPC sites that are still using 2.06 and some go back to other previous versions. It takes a long time to update." This is one of several problems that Shifter addresses via its operating system support for other version but Docker as a whole it too far outside the update cycle for many HPC centers.

Even with the right version, there is another weak point that was much discussed in enterprise Docker use cases, but comes with equal weight for HPC centers, especially since they tend to share large research systems with many users. You guessed it, it is security, and it is on this topic Jacobsen and his co-creator, Shane Canon, have put a great deal of effort. Before evolving into Shifter, Canon developed a tool called MyDock to secure Docker by requiring users to operate as themselves (Docker hands out contextual root access to the image, which is generally safe since users can only access things in the image but it involves some heavy mapping in of many volumes). This has been tested at scale in projects like the Dark Energy Survey and the work has landed inside Shifter.

While MyDock was useful and tested with some notable users, it did not scale up or scale out well enough to work efficiently on larger data-intensive systems, Jacobsen says. And further, during the MyDock and Docker era, it came down to Canon or another administrator to create and maintain all the images, so from a productivity standpoint, it wasn't scalable in that way either. The goal then, became to create a secure way for users to come in, create their environment and bring their software over and get up and running with all the security features of MyDock in place.

The security features for Shifter build onto what Docker (and then MyDock) does. Shifter gets around the security issues by using root privilege to set up the container but the processes are only ever executed within the container by that single user. "There is a controlled path for security management that meets the needs of HPC more directly than Docker," Jacobsen notes.

Of course, these are high performance computing centers we're talking about here, so what about the bottlenecks of the repositories and the networks? If a user wants to add one thousand images to start a job, how long does it take? It turns out, understanding some of the design constraints the Shifter creators bumped up against help explain this. What NERSC wanted from Shifter was simple in theory. Security, the correct versions, but further, they wanted to make sure users would not have to go through sys admins to get things rolling yet still be able to provide access to all the resources on the system (file system, high speed network, etc).

With Shifter, once the image is committed to the system, it's immutable, so in the cases where there is, for example, a 5 GB image, it goes into the system and across the parallel file system and the tuning features allow options for how many disk servers it will be spread across. That same file then gets mounted on all thousand nodes (if it's a thousand node calculation). Jacobsen said that the startup time performance for both Python and MPI jobs improved dramatically, going from tens of minutes to seconds. Shifter will be put to the test even further on the upcoming Cori supercomputer, which is set to hit the NERSC datacenter floor in its first phase this fall.

The point here is that the possibilities of cloud allowed some HPC centers to rethink their boundaries in terms of accessing compute capacity and containers took that one step further. It is now possible for HPC end users to "think freely" about both the infrastructure and applications—something that was far more difficult to do five years ago. With familiar workload management and middleware tools providing the "glue" between applications and infrastructure (no matter where its located) it stands to reason that the next wave of users will no longer think of their workloads as bound to place in the same way users just a few years ago did.

Chapter Five

The HPC to Machine Learning Cloud Leap

If there is one lesson that the big three public cloud providers teach, it is that there is no substitute for breadth and depth in software engineering. And ironically, as each one presents yet another new service that simplifies the life of IT operations, the rest of the world that then becomes dependent on these services and does not do its own thinking not only becomes a bit dumber, but also that much more dependent.

It's a brilliant business model, if you really consider it. And now that the big three clouds – Amazon Web Services, Microsoft Azure, and Google Cloud Platform – all have machine learning services, culled from their own experiences in peddling products and pushing ads over many years, that are fairly inexpensive, it is hard to imagine that millions of companies, of all sizes and around the world, won't eventually give these machine learning services a whirl. It sure beats trying to code it yourself and figuring out how to accelerate it with GPUs or FPGAs.

It is hard to draw a line between machine learning and predictive analytics, but all of these services lean a little more towards predictive analytics than they do towards the heavy-duty machine learning that is used to identify objects and people in images or video and write a description of what they are, or that powers the Siri and Cortana personal assistant services from Apple and Microsoft, or that controls a self-driving car. Machine learning sounds a lot cooler, to some ears at least, than does predictive analytics, and hence the term is bleeding over.

No matter what you call it, the new machine learning services from Amazon, Google, and Microsoft are definitely going to give predictive analytics software companies like SAS Institute, IBM, and Oracle a run for the money. Once again, services based on data and compute time fees and appealing to ease of use are pitting themselves against tried-and-true, best-of-breed analytics software with decades of evolution and use.

Amazon is the latest to trot out its machine learning services, and did so at its AWS Summit in San Francisco this year. Amazon Machine Learning (AML) is based on the company's own experiences with predictive analytics, which it has been dabbling with since it started out as an online bookseller in the dot-com era. Having invested untold sums in creating systems for supply chain management, fraud detection, and click prediction – this is a big one for online retailers – Amazon is not exposing its data visualization, machine learning modeling, and predictive analytics tools to the rest of the world through the AWS cloud. (Amazon uses machine learning to tell workers how to unpack a truck in the most expedient way possible to get the books into its warehouses and flowing back out to customers in other trucks, where ML is used to pack them.) All developers within Amazon have access to the ML stack and can embed it in their applications.

If AML seems a bit like giving away the online store (candy or otherwise), you can bet that whatever machine learning algorithms AWS is giving away, Amazon has kept some of the real jewels for itself. This is ever the way with the hyperscale titans.

AML starts with data, of course, and it designed to train against and do predictions against datasets that are no more than 100 GB in size. The data can be resident in the Relational Data Service with a MySQL backend, the S3 object store, or the Redshift data warehousing service. The latter two offer customers petabyte-scale storage if they want it, and it stands to reason that as customers embrace Amazon Machine Learning and try to train better models against larger datasets – more data is better than tweaking algorithms to create better predictive models faster, after all – that AWS will lift that 100 GB ceiling on dataset size. AWS says that the service does not actually pull data out of MySQL or Redshift, but rather uses the results of a query executed against those services. Any other data customers might want to use in their models can be stored in a CSV file and sucked into S3. AWS has data visualization tools to help show where fields are missing data in a dataset, and if 10 percent of the records in a dataset fail, then the machine learning service stops the model because the predictions generated won't be any good.

The machine learning service goes through the data and builds machine learning models, and they can be fine-tuned given more or better data sources, by making multiple passes over the data or applying different levels of regularization to the data. (Exactly how this all works is a bit of a mystery, and so by intention.) The idea is to train a dataset and then use it to make predictions based on new data streaming in. There is a batch API to have AML go through the whole dataset at one time and make predictions all at once, or you can use a real-time API to make predictions on demand for specific parts of data or specific predictions. AML can return a prediction request back over in about 100 milliseconds, which the company says is fast enough for web, mobile, and desktop applications; the IP address endpoint where a model sits on the AWS cloud can drive about 200 transactions per second. Amazon says that the AML service can be used to make billions of predictions per day, in real time, and it knows this because a variant of the service that has been running inside the online retailer is making more than 50 billion predictions per week (product recommendations and so forth) for the Amazon retail business.

One last thing: AML is sticky. You cannot export your machine learning models out of the AML service, and you cannot import any ML models created elsewhere into the AML service.

Target scenarios for AML are what you would expect. Fraud detection, demand forecasting, predictive customer support, and web click prediction. Customer service is another area, and the AML service could be used to analyze customer feedback from emails, forums, and telephone support transcripts to recommend corrective actions to product engineering and service teams as well as to connect new customers with similar issues to the appropriate customer support technicians who know about the problem and how to solve it.

As for pricing, the AML service is pretty straightforward. You pay for the local storage on S3, RDS, or Redshift for the data. The is costs another 42 cents per hour for AML to chew on that data to make the model; obviously, the more passes you make, the more money you spend. There is a supplemental charge for predictions on top of that , with batch predictions costing 10 cents per 1,000 predictions (rounded up to the nearest 1,000) and real-time predictions costing 1/10,000th of a penny each plus a an additional 1/1,000th of a penny for each 10 MB of reserved memory provisioned for the ML model as it is running. To make around 1 million predictions from a model if the model takes about 20 hours to run will cost just north of a hundred bucks.

Having all the World's Data Helps: Google's Machine Learning Cloud

At the dawn of the cloud computing revolution, the winners were determined in their ability to rule with an "iron" fist (the hardware) but over the next ten years, we will see that having an iron-fist basis for rule is far easier than ruling with nuanced, multi-layered intelligence–and it takes a special kind of leader to do that.

It takes a leader with boots on the ground for data collection, one who can deploy innumerable ears around every corner, ever-watching eyes that are tuned to the whole of citizenry, listening without discretion, silently but busily meshing all of that information into a consciousness of sorts–a collective knowledge base that can be combed, smoothed, and rolled out to appease different divisions in that land. While indeed this is a bit of dramatization for effect, this is exactly the kind of game of thrones that is happening just now among the giants of cloud. The iron throne is less a symbol than it used to be, the new seat of power is softer, changes position with the times, but always offers a 360 degree view.

In short, winter is coming for some of the most seasoned of the old guard.

Ten years ago, Amazon Web Services was differentiated in the fact that it had no real competitors that were able to tap into the economies of scale that continue to make that business what it is today. Through partnerships, hard work to roll out in-depth use cases from top companies, and consistent improvements to the infrastructure, security, and code base, AWS grew to become the behemoth it is today, while others, including Microsoft, IBM, Rackspace, and more followed behind, carving out markets where AWS left off and maintaining them through ever-slimmer price, technology, and code wars.

One can make the argument now, however, that the next platform for emerging cloud applications is rooted in far more than the infrastructure base that propelled those public cloud efforts. The stack itself is shifting and while many businesses will continue to scale their applications on AWS, Azure, and elsewhere, a new code and cultural base is firming up around machine learning. And despite what we are covering in these early stages of its growth and potential in enterprise, it goes far beyond more consumer-geared services like voice recognition for mobile apps or facial recognition to allow fast classification of an individual's photo library. Machine learning is, in fact, the next platform.

Herein is what separates the first big wave of Infrastructure as a Service successes — the last decade (and first real decade) of cloud computing from what is next. Over the next decade, the infrastructure will continue to be the "easy" part and the real defining factors of success will be the ability to capture, train, and model data for users and from users using machine learning.

Google aims its Prediction API service at similar targets as AML and Azure ML, and it has been available since the fall of 2011 as a part of its App Engine platform cloud.

The training size of the Prediction API is capped at 2.5 GB, and files are loaded into the Google Storage service. Google says that it usually takes from minutes to a couple of hours to train a dataset. Once it is trained and is running against new data, it takes on the order of 200 milliseconds to generate a prediction.

Google's freebie service allows data scientists to do 100 predictions per day and train against a mere 5 MB of data per day; there is a lifetime cap of 20,000 predictions. For the paid Predictive API service, Google has a minimum $10 per month fee, which covers up to 10,000 predictions, and it costs 50 cents per 1,000 predictions after that. It costs 2/10ths of a cent per MB for training datasets, plus additional fees for streaming updates into the dataset. The for-fee service has a cap of 2 million predictions per day, and Google wants to be notified if data scientists want to get above 40,000 predictions per day. Charges do not reflect the Google Storage costs for live datasets.

At the NEXT 2016 conference, Google's Eric Schmidt touched on one of the biggest advantages Google has in that next decade of cloud ahead. It's not infrastructure or software—and it's not even as simple as pure "data" to work with. It's the crowdsourced intelligence—an evolving, streaming pool of it—to create smarter systems from the top down that users at all levels can tap into, retrain, alter, and output for their own purposes. It is the next evolution of cloud.

This concept of crowdsourcing data that can lead to better, smarter, wider-scale training is at the heart of Google's competitive advantage for the next decade of cloud, Schmidt says. "I'm convinced that a rapid evaluation model, Google Cloud Platform, machine learning, and crowdsourcing will be the basis of every big IPO win in the next five years." This will be an evolution similar to the arrival

> "Google Cloud Platform is timed perfectly for what's going to happen next. This platform is not the end, it's the bottom layer—there's something above it. That thing is machine learning, both narrow AI and general AI. It's the next transformation. The programming paradigm changes. Instead of programming a computer, you teach a computer to learn something and it does what you want. This is a fundamental change for programming."

of apps—putting exactly what is required in front of the user with intelligence built in and with the infrastructure hidden behind so many layers of abstraction that the experience is seamless. As Schmidt compares, this is much like the evolution of the automobile industry—from the early days, to the clutch, to the self-driving car of the future.

Schmidt says the best way to prepare for this transform is to start building on top of Linux, Google Cloud Platform, and Kubernetes. On the development side, to work with modern, scalable, portable languages like Go, Python, node.js, java, and build in the Google App Engine. But at the top of this list, he says, it's a matter of getting comfortable with TensorFlow, which will be at the heart of Google's (and many other enterprises, in his estimation) machine learning and analytical strategies over the next five years.

With the rollout of the company's new machine learning platform its own cloud, there is a flag in the sand planted that should set AWS, Microsoft with its Azure offering, and of course, companies with advanced machine learning and the cloudy infrastructure to host on like IBM, scrambling. This is, as noted earlier, because unlike those other companies, Google has the crowdsourcing services (not to mention appeal) through its many photo, voice, and text-based services that the others do not. And it is harnessing this crowdsourcing to power new services like those listed here.

THE STATE OF HPC CLOUD

"Over the past few years, we've been building machine learning into everything we do", says Jeff Dean, a Google Fellow in the Systems Infrastructure Group and lead of the Google Brain project. *This is why the company's Android speech recognition system works so well, why their translation services are so far-reaching and relatively accurate, and why their photo face and object recognition with classification is so seamless. These are again, crowdsourced services—the ability of Google's services to provide the most rich archive and streaming source of data to make much smarter machines and more advanced deep learning capabilities. The other clouds ruled with (big) iron fists before, Google will take a softer approach (software).*

Armed with TensorFlow to allow sophisticated deep learning as a fully managed service, the next decade of cloud could be very different, indeed—not to mention the next generation of analytics. We've moved from the era of figuring out what to do with so much data using variations on the same old tools (and some new frameworks like MapReduce and Hadoop) to taking a quantum leap ahead by letting that data figure itself out, at least in theory. And that is a big deal—one that could threaten the current cloud hegemony, which does not have the full-stack focus and crowdsource-able services that mighty Google has.

THE STATE OF HPC CLOUD

Although TensorFlow is just rising at the end of 2015, Schmidt believes this is the foundation for the next generation of Google's ability to reach farther into what cloud can offer for large-scale enterprise with complex analytical workloads. It is the beginning of the next wave of applications and cloud use cases–and quite possibility, for Google's own position as a force to be reckoned with for the Fortune 500s who took their first steps with AWS or others and have hitherto remained in those environments.

Not long ago, as we remarked here on the end of the first decade of AWS, even if it was in the context of very-large scale applications, the focus was on the evolution of the infrastructure and the related tools and services that hooked into it. That was a fitting look back since the cloud's first decade was strongly rooted in these "base" concerns of security, networking, and of course, the iron required to power an exploding range of user applications. There is little doubt that AWS pioneered the cloud as we know it, with additional elements being thrown in by other companies who lacked the same initial incentive to begin renting out spare infrastructure (versus building datacenters simply for hosting cloud-based services).

With all due respect to that effort—and what lies ahead for AWS and its companions in the cloud space, armed with crowdsourced data and the machine learning and deep learning frameworks to do something profoundly useful with it, bolstering new and existing services, Google is set to give the cloud camps a fast dash for their money. This could very well be the year that Google's cloud finds its footing in a way it hasn't before with large-scale enterprise, who took their first tenuous steps to the public cloud (often via hybrid models) with Amazon and will take some convincing to be wrenched free after all the initial fear, cost, risk, and cultural changes that came with the shift away from purely on-prem infrastructure.

What will get companies to take another look at their cloud options is no longer the hardware. It is roughly equivalent—and one can expect Google to take further efforts to bolster its range of "instances" as AWS did once it realized that capturing certain markets meant a diversity of memory, acceleration, CPU, and networking options. What will make them look again is the one area of differentiation that is very hard for most companies to create or emulate—the next generation of smart analytical capabilities. Capabilities that are so smart, tuned, and aware that the oversight required, outside of the beginning effort, will be game-changing, at least in Google's view.

Microsoft Azure Imports Machine Learning Expertise From Amazon

When Microsoft wanted to build its own machine learning stack and expose it as a service on its Azure cloud, it went straight to the top and hired away Joseph Sirosh from Amazon in July 2013. (The commute didn't change much for him, presumably.)

Microsoft's Azure ML service went into beta last June, and includes many of the ML algorithms that the company uses to run its Bing search engine and Xbox gaming sites. Microsoft also allows for algorithms written in the open source R statistical language and in Python to be woven into the Azure ML stack, and developers can share the ML algorithms they create for free through a gallery and a for a fee through a marketplace. The recent acquisition by Microsoft of Revolution Analytics, which has radically boosted the performance of the R statistics engine, no doubt will help bolster the Azure ML service.

Carnegie Mellon University is a customer, and is using Azure ML to do predictive maintenance on its facilities, and ThyssenKrupp is using the service to do a similar task on the elevators it installs in skyscrapers. Pier 1 Imports is another customer using Azure ML, and in this case it is using the service to do predictive modelling of customer purchases.

Microsoft is only peddling the Azure ML service out of its South Central US region at the moment. There is a free tier that comes with a maximum of 100 modules per experiment. (A module is an algorithm or a source of data or a data transformation operation in Azure ML speak.) The Machine Learning Studio tool that is part of the service can train on a dataset that is 10 GB or smaller, but predictive analytics can be run against a Hive data warehouse layer running on hosted HDInsight Hadoop services or against queries from the Azure SQL Database service. If you have datasets larger than 10 GB, you can partition it and then run training sessions on pieces and merge the results. The freebie version of the Azure ML service also caps out with a 1 hour maximum on the dataset training (what Microsoft calls an experiment) and has a maximum of 10 GB of storage space; it runs on a single node and with the staging API to the web throttled back.

The standard Azure ML service, which has a fee associated with it, has an unlimited number of modules, runs on multiple nodes, and doesn't have API caps. Azure ML costs $9.99 per seat per month for data scientists, plus $1 per hour for model training and then $2 per compute hour to feed results out to APIs for application integration plus 50 cents per 1,000 API transactions. You have to pay for your larger dataset storage as well, of course, just like on Amazon Machine Learning.

IBM SoftLayer and Cognos/SPSS can be expected to move next toward machine learning in the cloud. SAS Institute already has its own SaaS analytics, but could partner to get wider exposure, particularly with any of the big public clouds and maybe even smaller players like Rackspace Hosting. That said, Rackspace increasingly likes open software, so a SAS partnership might not make sense. But grabbing the open source R tools and maybe Apache Mahout or Spark MLlib for Hadoop and crafting its own ML service might.

The one thing that those above lack, at least to the greater extent of Amazon and Microsoft, are previous investments in the hardware required for high performance computing. In short, the early investments made by the world's largest cloud builders are paying off, particularly in terms of GPU options. These are still early days for machine learning and deep learning in the cloud, but at this early stage, the companies with the most investments in HPC hardware and tooling will be the most likely to win mindshare among the big players. However, we turn our eye again to the idea that specialization matters. It is not unconceivable that users will pass on the big players and go with specialty clouds with their own ASICs or other hardware configurations designed to work well with key deep learning or machine learning libraries. We have definitely seen an uptick in interest for custom hardware this year, and seeing that extend to clouds would not be surprising.

What is good for HPC in the cloud has been great for remote machine learning as well. This is the type of symbiotic development that makes all of bleeding edge computing worthwhile and interesting if not hugely profitable…yet.

Chapter Six

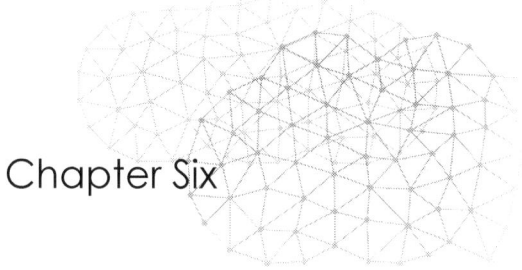

The Truth About HPC Cloud—And What's Next

By Addison Snell, Intersect360 Research

This book is in the cloud. It is about the cloud. It is of the cloud.

The cloud enables us. The cloud empowers us. The cloud surrounds us. Its transformative power has spawned new businesses and transformed old ones. It has turned internet heavyweights into hyperscale giants, mammoth cloud providers spending—in some cases— over $1 billion per year on IT.

When cloud first burst onto the scene—less than a decade ago, though it can be hard to remember back that far—we argued over the definition of "cloud." What was it? What was it for? Who was using it, and why? Different perspectives competed, and still do. Cloud as an architecture: "This is my IT infrastructure. It is a cloud." Cloud as a delivery mechanism: "We don't have the resources in house. We run our applications in the cloud." Cloud as a safety net: "Protect your data forever in the cloud."

Today the definitional debate has waned. There's no one left who wants to hear another explanation of what the cloud is and what it can do for them. And yet, there are distinct business models offered by cloud computing, public, private and hybrid.

There are myriad cloud service providers out there, all competing for your business. Combined with smaller providers, application specialists, and scientific collaboration sites, there are hundreds of public clouds available. They offer you the ability to outsource any portion of your IT infrastructure or workload, scaled to the size required, and adjustable over time.

Sure, you have to pay a premium to cover management and overhead. And if you can use the majority of the capacity you buy, it isn't necessarily any cheaper to outsource, relative to managing infrastructure internally. But for many users, cloud computing is worth it.

And it has a major role in the market.

Even within HPC, a market that has been resistant to it, we see major growth potential for cloud. In addition to bursting for short-term additions to peak capability, cloud provides an on-ramp for organizations that are moving into HPC for the first time. There have always been application consultants to help manage workloads, and now the infrastructure can be outsourced along with the expertise.

If the promise of cloud computing is overblown, it because of the amplification it gets from its loyal converts, enterprises who have found liberation and agility in outsourcing IT. There will still be segments of the market where cloud computing doesn't make economic or operational sense, and even some workloads and data sets for which enterprises reintegrate workloads, bringing them back on-premise out of the cloud.

Even if the cloud isn't the answer for all of IT, we can still look to cloud computing to play a major role in future advancements. Major IT touchpoints, including Internet of Things, mobile computing, and augmented reality, all have ties to cloud computing as a back-end enabler of computation at scale.

Among all the possibilities for evolutionary computing, one stands out brightly as being truly revolutionary: artificial intelligence. Once the stuff of science fiction, special cases of artificial intelligence have already made it into the market, including image recognition, speech recognition, and natural language processing; the ability to play complex games like go or poker at a championship level; and the introduction of the first self-driving cars.

The recent advancements in AI have largely been based on machine learning, wherein the computer is trained over very large data sets (these are all renditions of the letter H; these are not) and then programmed to make inferences about the next bit of data it is given. Because of the vast amounts of computation required for training in machine learning, the spearhead of AI research to date has been represented by hyperscale computing companies, such as Google, Facebook, Apple, Baidu, Amazon, and IBM. These companies utilize their massive cloud infrastructures to fuel the training cycles for machine learning.

Current implementations of AI are only the beginning of the beginning. Phrases like "tip of the iceberg" or "point of the spear" are inadequate; they are more akin to hearing the first strains of the orchestra tuning up before a symphony: only the merest of hints as to what the sound is capable of becoming. The possible advancements in healthcare are often touted, and they are true, but the immediate potential is even greater in less marketable arenas, such as finance, where machine learning can be applied in dimensions from fraud detection to pricing. (As appetizing as personalized medicine sounds, you might see your own personalized interest rate first.)

In a sense, AI lies at an intersection between the HPC market and the hyperscale market. It certainly demands tremendous resources, and it frequently involves the use of high-performance components, such as faster interconnects or processing elements. However, it is a "scale out" type of application more than "scale up"—all those training bits of data are independent from one another, unlike, say, the air molecules in an aerodynamics simulation—and the majority of the resources spent on it now are on the hyperscale side.

There are other motivations for this besides architecture. The cloud provider is not researching AI strictly magnanimously. Consider the end game for, say, AI in medicine. Even the inference portion will need to be linked at some level to the data that provides an ongoing feedback loop of training. Will we put mid-range HPC clusters in every doctor's office? No. The client app in the doctor's office will talk to the cloud. *The* cloud. Which cloud? Probably the cloud belonging to the company that designed the application, the company that did the machine learning training. The cloud provider that owns it. It's in the cloud.

The truth is, cloud computing is here to stay, and it is growing, specifically because it represents a new paradigm that introduces more capabilities to more people. But it is not a panacea that will overwhelm the IT landscape. Cloud will not fully displace on-premise, but it will remain an extended part of the infrastructure—the hybrid cloud, if you will—in most forward-looking enterprises. And it will enable fabulous new applications, things that we have dreamt of, and even things we have not.

The true leaders in adopting cloud computing are not the organizations that heuristically push everything off-premise based on the faith that life is better in The Cloud. Rather, the true leaders are the ones who see past the platitudes to determine which clouds to adopt, when and where, and for what.

With a well thought out strategy, cloud computing can help transform an enterprise, introducing more capabilities, streamlining operations, or delivering more return for an optimal investment. There are a lot of clouds to choose from, ready to scale to any level of need, with utility pricing plans that make financial sense for a lot of workloads. And that's no lie.

References and Resources

Abid, M. R. (2016). HPC (High-Performance the Computing) for Big Data on Cloud: Opportunities and Challenges. *International Journal of Computer Theory and Engineering*, 8(5), 423.

Atif, M., Kobayashi, R., Menadue, B. J., Lin, C. Y., Sanderson, M., & Williams, A. (2016). Breaking HPC Barriers with the 56GbE Cloud. *Procedia Computer Science*, 93, 3-11.

Black, Doug (2015, August) The need for a new HPC architectural direction: Revolution or evolution? http://www.nextplatform.com/2015/08/10/the-need-for-a-new-hpc-architectural-direction-revolution-or-evolution/

Benedict, S. (2013). Performance issues and performance analysis tools for HPC cloud applications: a survey. *Computing*, 95(2), 89-108.

Chen, H., Wu, S., Jin, H., Chen, W., Zhai, J., Luo, Y., & Wang, X. (2016). A survey of cloud resource management for complex engineering applications. *Frontiers of Computer Science*, 1-15.

Chrzeszczyk, J., Howard, A., Chrzeszczyk, A., Swift, B., Davis, P., Low, J., ... & Ban, K. (2016). InfiniCloud 2.0: distributing High Performance Computing across continents. *Supercomputing frontiers and innovations*, 3(2), 54-71.

Conway, Steve (2015, March) When data needs more firepower: The HPC, analytics convergence. http://www.nextplatform.com/2015/03/04/when-data-needs-more-firepower-the-hpc-analytics-convergence/

Da Cunha Rodrigues, G., Calheiros, R. N., Guimaraes, V. T., Santos, G. L. D., de Carvalho, M. B., Granville, L. Z., ... & Buyya, R. (2016, April). Monitoring of cloud computing environments: concepts, solutions, trends, and future directions. In *Proceedings of the 31st Annual ACM Symposium on Applied Computing* (pp. 378-383). ACM.

de Carvalho Silva, J., & de Carvalho Junior, F. H. (2016, September). A Platform of Scientific Workflows for Orchestration of Parallel Components in a Cloud of High Performance Computing Applications. In *Brazilian Symposium on Programming Languages* (pp. 156-170). Springer International Publishing.

Dragan, I., Fortis, T. F., & Neagul, M. (2016). Exposing HPC services in the Cloud: the CloudLightning Approach. *Scalable Computing: Practice and Experience, 17*(4), 323-330.

el Khaldi, F., Ahouangonou, C., Niess, M., & David, O. (2016). Cloud Based HPC for Innovative Virtual Prototyping Methodology: Automotive Applications. *Transportation Research Procedia, 14,* 993-1002.

Emeras, J., Varrette, S., & Bouvry, P. (2016). Amazon Elastic Compute Cloud (EC2) vs. in-House HPC Platform: a Cost Analysis. In *Proc. of the 9th IEEE Intl. Conf. on Cloud Computing (CLOUD 2016).* IEEE Computer Society.

Freniere, C., Pathak, A., Raessi, M., & Khanna, G. (2016). The Feasibility of Amazon's Cloud Computing Platform for Parallel, GPU-Accelerated, Multiphase-Flow Simulations. *Computing in Science & Engineering, 18*(5), 68-77.

Gad, R., Pickartz, S., Süß, T., Nagel, L., Lankes, S., & Brinkmann, A. (2016, June). Accelerating Application Migration in HPC. In *International Conference on High Performance Computing* (pp. 663-673). Springer International Publishing.

Galante, G., De Bona, L. C. E., Mury, A. R., Schulze, B., & da Rosa Righi, R. (2016). An Analysis of Public Clouds Elasticity in the Execution of Scientific Applications: a Survey. *Journal of Grid Computing, 14*(2), 193-216.

Gannon, D., Fay, D., Green, D., Takeda, K., & Yi, W. (2014, June). Science in the cloud: lessons from three years of research projects on microsoft azure. In *Proceedings of the 5th ACM workshop on scientific cloud computing* (pp. 1-8). ACM.

Gentzsch, W., & Yenier, B. (2016). Novel Software Containers for Engineering and Scientific Simulations in the Cloud. *International Journal of Grid and High Performance Computing (IJGHPC), 8*(1), 38-49.

Hemsoth, N. (2016, March). Ten Years of AWS and a Status Check for HPC Clouds. http://www.nextplatform.com/2016/03/15/ten-years-aws-status-check-hpc-clouds/

Hemsoth, N (2016, May) ANSYS Leaps HPC Cloud Software License Barrier. http://www.nextplatform.com/2015/05/07/ansys-leaps-hpc-cloud-software-license-barrier/

Hemsoth, Nicole (2015, June) The cloud versus HPC cluster cost conundrum. http://www.nextplatform.com/2015/06/03/the-hpc-cloud-versus-cluster-cost-conundrum/

Hemsoth, Nicole. (2016, August) Specialized supercomputing cloud turns eye to machine learning. http://www.nextplatform.com/2016/08/23/specialized-supercomputing-cloud-turns-eye-machine-learning/

Hemsoth, Nicole (2016, May) IBM extends GPU capabilities, targets machine learning. http://www.nextplatform.com/2016/05/19/ibm-extends-gpu-cloud-capabilities-targets-machine-learning/

Hemsoth, Nicole (2016, January) Google playing swift catch up in life sciences cloud. http://www.nextplatform.com/2016/01/12/google-playing-swift-catch-up-in-life-sciences-cloud/

Hemsoth, Nicole (2015, November) FPGAs glimmer on the HPC horizon, glint in the hyperscale sun. http://www.nextplatform.com/2015/11/17/fpgas-glimmer-on-the-hpc-horizon-glint-in-hyperscale-sun/

Hemsoth, Nicole (2015, November) A clever approach to cultivating the HPC stack. http://www.nextplatform.com/2015/11/12/a-clever-approach-to-cultivating-the-hpc-stack/

Hemsoth, Nicole (2015, September) Shifter expands container capabilities for HPC. http://www.nextplatform.com/2015/09/23/shifter-expands-container-capabilities-for-hpc/

Hemsoth, Nicole (2015, August) New network architecture bridges supercomputer, cloud divides. http://www.nextplatform.com/2015/08/13/new-network-architecture-bridges-supercomputer-cloud-divides/

Hemsoth, Nicole (2015, September) Intel HPC lead outlines commercial supercomputing roadmap. http://www.nextplatform.com/2015/09/14/intel-hpc-lead-outlines-commercial-supercomputing-roadmap/

Hemsoth, Nicole (2015, May) Rescale's political stance boosts cloud based supercomputing. http://www.nextplatform.com/2015/05/27/rescales-political-stance-boosts-cloud-based-supercomputing/

Hemsoth, Nicole (2015, May) A cloudy outlook for oil and gas simulations. http://www.nextplatform.com/2015/05/14/a-cloudy-outlook-for-oil-and-gas-simulations/

Hemsoth, Nicole (2015, March) FPGA market floats future on the cloud. http://www.nextplatform.com/2015/03/24/fpga-market-floats-future-on-the-cloud/

Hemsoth, Nicole (2015, March) HPC schedulers snap to Docker. http://www.nextplatform.com/2015/03/23/hpc-schedulers-snap-to-docker/

Hemsoth, Nicole (2015, February) Risk modeling upstart finds edge with GPU clouds. http://www.nextplatform.com/2015/02/22/risk-modeling-upstart-finds-edge-with-gpu-clouds/

Hemsoth, Nicole (2015, June) IBM opens its EDA platform to startup chipmakers. http://www.nextplatform.com/2015/06/23/ibm-opens-its-eda-platform-to-startup-chipmakers/

Hemsoth, Nicole (2015, September) Google, Cycle Computing pair for broad genomics effort. http://www.nextplatform.com/2015/09/08/google-cycle-computing-pair-for-broad-genomics-effort/

Hemsoth, Nicole (2016, June) Life sciences clouds raise more cluster questions. http://www.nextplatform.com/2015/06/09/life-sciences-clouds-raise-more-cluster-questions/

Iserte, S., Clemente-Castelló, F. J., Castelló, A., Mayo, R., & Quintana-Ortı́, E. S. (2016). Enabling GPU Virtualization in Cloud Environments.

Katz, D. S., & Zhou, X. (2016). Leading-edge research in cluster, cloud, and grid computing: Best papers from the IEEE/ACM CCGrid 2015 conference. *Future Generation Computer Systems*.

Keahey, K., Raicu, I., Chard, K., & Nicolae, B. (2016). Guest Editors Introduction: Special Issue on Scientific Cloud Computing. *IEEE Transactions on Cloud Computing*, 4(1), 4-5.

Kim, I., Jung, J. Y., DeLuca, T. F., Nelson, T. H., & Wall, D. P. (2012). Cloud computing for comparative genomics with windows azure platform. *Evolutionary Bioinformatics*, 8, 527.

Kirkley, John (2016, June) System software, orchestration gets an OpenHPC boost. http://www.nextplatform.com/2016/06/29/system-software-orchestration-gets-openhpc-boost/

Lakshminarayanan, R., & Ramalingam, R. (2016). Usage of Cloud Computing Simulators and Future Systems For Computational Research. *arXiv preprint arXiv:1605.00085*.

Lee, E. K., Viswanathan, H., & Pompili, D. (2016). Proactive thermal-aware resource management in virtualized HPC cloud datacenters.

Llopis, P., Blas, J. G., & Isaila, F. (2016). Work in progress about enhancing the programmability and energy efficiency of storage in HPC and cloud environments. *Computing Systems (NESUS PhD 2016) Timisoara, Romania*, 79.

Lockwood, Glenn (2015, March) DNA sequencing: Not quite HPC yet. http://www.nextplatform.com/2015/03/03/dna-sequencing-not-quite-hpc-yet/

Mashayekhi, O., Shah, C., Qu, H., Lim, A., & Levis, P. (2016). Distributed Graphical Simulation in the Cloud. *arXiv preprint arXiv:1606.01966*.

Morgan, Timothy Prickett (2015, April) Why cloud is taking over datacenter spending. http://www.nextplatform.com/2015/04/22/why-cloud-is-taking-over-datacenter-spending/

Morgan, Timothy Prickett (2015, October). How many other public clouds will be vaporized? http://www.nextplatform.com/2015/10/22/how-many-other-public-clouds-will-be-vaporized/

Morgan, Timothy Prickett (2015, October) Transition to platforms, cloud tough for IBM. http://www.nextplatform.com/2015/10/20/transition-to-platforms-cloud-tough-for-ibm/

Morgan, Timothy Prickett (2015, October) IBM back in HPC with Power systems clusters. http://www.nextplatform.com/2015/10/08/ibm-back-in-hpc-with-power-systems-lc-clusters/

Morgan, Timothy Prickett (2015, October) Cloudy infrastructure drives datacenter spending growth. http://www.nextplatform.com/2015/10/02/cloudy-infrastructure-drives-datacenter-spending-growth/

Morgan, Timothy Prickett (2016, May) How big is the ecosystem growing on clouds? http://www.nextplatform.com/2016/05/02/big-ecosystem-growing-clouds/

Morgan, Timothy Prickett (2016, April) Hyperscalers and clouds on the Xeon bleeding edge. http://www.nextplatform.com/2016/04/13/hyperscalers-clouds-xeon-bleeding-edge/

Morgan, Timothy Prickett (2016, June) HPC spending outpaces the IT market, and will continue to. http://www.nextplatform.com/2016/06/22/hpc-spending-outpaces-market-will-continue/

Morgan, Timothy Prickett (2015, November) HPC Spending Expands with Clouds and Data. http://www.nextplatform.com/2015/11/17/hpc-spending-on-the-rise/

Morgan, Timothy Prickett (2015, August) Dell leverages hyperscale expertise for HPC, clouds and enterprise. http://www.nextplatform.com/2015/08/24/dell-leverages-hyperscale-expertise-for-hpc-clouds-and-enterprise/

Morgan, Timothy Prickett (2016, September) Amazon gets sources about GPU compute on clouds. http://www.nextplatform.com/2016/09/30/amazon-gets-serious-gpu-compute-clouds/

Morgan, Timothy Prickett (2016, September) IBM builds bridge between private and public power clouds. http://www.nextplatform.com/2016/09/21/ibm-builds-bridge-private-public-power-clouds/

Morgan, Timothy Prickett (2016, August) HPE expands reach with SGI buy http://www.nextplatform.com/2016/08/11/hpe-expands-hpc-reach-sgi-buy/

Morgan, Timothy Prickett (2016, August) Taking a long view of HPC and beyond. http://www.nextplatform.com/2016/08/05/taking-long-view-hpc-beyond/

Morgan, Timothy (2015, July) GPU computing still nascent on public clouds. http://www.nextplatform.com/2015/07/08/gpu-computing-still-nascent-on-public-clouds/

Petri, I., Li, H., Rezgui, Y., Chunfeng, Y., Yuce, B., & Jayan, B. (2016). A HPC based cloud model for real-time energy optimisation. *Enterprise Information Systems*, *10*(1), 108-128.

Posey, B. (2016). *Dynamic HPC clusters within Amazon Web Services (AWS)*.

Richter, H. (2016). About the Suitability of Clouds in High-Performance Computing. *arXiv preprint arXiv:1601.01910*.

Sieslack, Nages (2015, April) An insider's view of financial modeling on HPC systems. http://www.nextplatform.com/2015/04/21/an-insiders-view-of-financial-modeling-on-hpc-systems/

Snell, Addison (2016, September) The three great lies of cloud computing. http://www.nextplatform.com/2016/09/21/three-great-lies-cloud-computing/

Teich, Paul (2016, July) HPC flows into hyperscale with Dell Triton http://www.nextplatform.com/2016/07/18/hpc-flows-hyperscale-dell-triton/

Tudoran, R., Costan, A., Antoniu, G., & Bougé, L. (2012, April). A performance evaluation of Azure and Nimbus clouds for scientific applications. In *Proceedings of the 2nd International Workshop on Cloud Computing Platforms* (p. 4). ACM.

Wu, D., Terpenny, J., & Schaefer, D. (2016). Digital design and manufacturing on the cloud: A review of software and services. *Artificial Intelligence for Engineering Design, Analysis and Manufacturing, Cambridge University Press*, 1-15.

Zhang, J., Lu, X., & Panda, D. K. (2016, August). High Performance MPI Library for Container-Based HPC Cloud on InfiniBand Clusters. In *Parallel Processing (ICPP), 2016 45th International Conference on* (pp. 268-277). IEEE.

Made in the USA
San Bernardino, CA
30 January 2017